A2 Sociology
UNIT 4

AQA

Module 4: Religion

Joan Garrod and Tony Lawson

Series Editor: Joan Garrod

For Robin

Philip Allan Updates
Market Place
Deddington
Oxfordshire
OX15 0SE

tel: 01869 338652
fax: 01869 337590
e-mail: sales@philipallan.co.uk
www.philipallan.co.uk

This Guide has been written specifically to support students preparing for the AQA A2 Sociology Unit 4 examination. The content has been neither approved nor endorsed by AQA and remains the sole responsibility of the authors.

Printed by Raithby, Lawrence and Co. Ltd, Leicester

Contents

Introduction

■ ■ ■

Content Guidance

■ ■ ■

Questions and Answers

Introduction

About this guide

This unit guide is aimed at students taking the AQA A2 Sociology course. It covers the topic of **Religion**, which is examined within Unit 4 (SCY4) and is one of the three choices of topic in the module, along with Power and Politics and World Sociology. This topic is designed to give you a good understanding of the importance of religion to individuals and to society as a whole, as well as of the different types of religious organisations and beliefs and how these have changed over time. There are three sections in this unit guide:

- **Introduction** — this provides advice on how to use the guide, an explanation of the skills required in A2 Sociology and suggestions for effective revision. It concludes with guidance on how to succeed in the unit test.
- **Content Guidance** — this provides you with an overview of what is included in the specification for Religion. It is designed to make you aware of what you should know before the unit test.
- **Questions and Answers** — this offers some exam-type questions on religion for you to try, together with some sample answers at grade-A and grade-C levels. Examiner's comments are included to show how marks are awarded at A2.

How to use the guide

To benefit most from this guide, you need to use different parts of it at different stages during your course of study. Initially you should refer to the Introduction and have a look at the Content Guidance sections. As you progress through the topic, you should refer to the relevant section of the Content Guidance to ensure that you have understood the main concepts used. To get the best out of the Question and Answer section, you should attempt to answer some questions as you go along. This will help you to consolidate the knowledge you have gained and organise your understanding of the topic in a systematic fashion. As you move into revision mode for the unit test, attempt the questions you have not done as part of an active revision strategy.

To use these questions and answers effectively, you have to be honest. Having studied the question carefully, you should attempt to answer each part (or the whole thing if it is an essay response) yourself, without looking first at the example answers given. This is important: by comparing your answers and the specimen answers you will understand what you might have done better and so improve your performance. When you have completed your answers, study the grade-A candidate's answer and the examiner's comments to see where you might have been able to make improvements, giving particular thought to the different skills that you have to demonstrate. You should also look at the grade-C answer and, with the guidance of the examiner's comments, rewrite it so that it would gain an A-grade mark.

These tasks are time-consuming, so forward planning is essential. Find out the date of the Unit 4 exam and draw up a timetable that allows you to get all the activities done in good time. This will also help you to fit these activities in with your other revision tasks.

In addition to using the questions to develop your examination skills, you could draw on the answers as a source of revision material. Simply reading through the grade-A candidate's answers should provide you with useful reminders of important sociological material. Remember, however, that in the exam you must answer the question that is on your paper, not try to reproduce the specimen answer.

The A2 specification

The aims of the A2 Sociology course are to enable you to:
- acquire knowledge and a critical understanding of contemporary social processes and structures
- appreciate the significance of theoretical and conceptual issues in sociological debate
- understand sociological methodology and a range of research methods
- reflect on your own experience of the social world you live in
- develop skills that enhance your ability to participate more effectively in adult life

Examinable skills

A2 Sociology papers are designed to test certain defined skills which are referred to as 'Assessment Objectives' in the specification. You will already have been tested in these Assessment Objectives in your AS Sociology module examinations, but the weighting for each of the two Assessment Objectives (AO1 and AO2) is different for the A2 Sociology specification. Over the three modules of A2, the proportion of marks given to AO1 (knowledge and understanding) is 45% and for AO2 (identification, analysis, interpretation and evaluation) is 55%. This means that you are required to demonstrate more sophisticated skills of analysis and evaluation at A2 than for AS. You will need to show a more critical, reflective and evaluative approach to method-ological issues, to the nature of sociological enquiry and to sociological debates, drawing on a wide and varied range of sources.

Module 4 constitutes 15% of the total marks available for the whole of AS and A2, but the Assessment Objective weighting for Module 4 is 6% for AO1 skills and 9% for AO2 skills. This shows the proportion of marks allocated to each of the two Assessment Objectives. Three-fifths of the 60 marks available in the Module 4 unit test are awarded for the demonstration of AO2 skills and only two-fifths for AO1 skills.

Assessment Objective 1

O1 involves the connected skills of knowledge and understanding. The examiners will be looking for clear evidence that you have appropriate, accurate knowledge and a good understanding of the sociological material in the topic you are studying. You will find an account of the basic knowledge in Religion in the Content Guidance section, but remember that it is not enough to be able to reproduce knowledge learned by rote in the examination. You must also show that you have understood it and can select the most appropriate information and use it in a meaningful way to answer the specific question set.

You also need to demonstrate knowledge and understanding of the core themes of the specification:

- socialisation, culture and identity
- social differentiation, power and stratification

These themes run through various elements of the AS and A2 courses, including the topic of Religion. The Content Guidance section indicates where aspects of the themes are dealt with. All the topics that are studied in A-level Sociology, including Religion, also cover what are called 'Integral Elements' — that is, information and approaches that make connections between different substantive areas, sociological theories, perspectives and methods, and the design and evaluation of research methods.

The AQA A-level specification in sociology requires a good knowledge and under-standing of a range of sociological methods and sources, in particular of the relation-ship between theory and methods. This includes the way that sociologists:

- acquire primary and secondary data through observation, asking questions and using documents
- analyse qualitative and quantitative data using appropriate concepts
- design and execute sociological research
- are influenced by ethical considerations

You will also need to demonstrate sociological thinking by making links between concepts and theories and applying them to the substantive area you have chosen to study, in this case, religion. Sociological thought covers:

- social order, social control and social change
- conflict and consensus
- social structure and social action
- macro and micro perspectives
- the nature of social facts
- the role of values
- the relationship between sociology and social policy

Finally, regarding the quality of written communication, the relevant AO1 skills include the ability to use:

- a style of writing appropriate for transmitting complex information

- specialist vocabulary such as sociological concepts when appropriate
- accurate spelling, punctuation and grammar to ensure that the meaning is clear

Assessment Objective 2

Assessment Objective 2 (AO2) covers 'identification, analysis, interpretation and evaluation'. More marks are given for AO2 skills than for AO1, so be prepared to be show that you have learnt how to:

- select appropriate pieces of sociological knowledge and arguments and distinguish between facts and opinion (**identification**)
- break down sociological studies and debates into their component parts — concepts, perspective, method, findings, conclusion, strengths and weaknesses (**analysis**)
- examine material such as statistics, tables, graphs and research findings to identify trends and establish their meaning and importance (**interpretation**)
- assess the relevance and importance of sociological studies and debates, conveying their strengths and weaknesses and coming to a conclusion about them (**evaluation**)

Evaluation is a particularly important skill at A2 and you should try to develop the habit of evaluation as you go through your course. For every piece of sociological research and every perspective that you examine, try to establish a minimum of two strengths and two weaknesses and to ask questions such as 'Why should I believe this?', 'What evidence is there for this viewpoint?', 'Are there any counter-arguments?' and 'Who says so?' Gradually you will develop the ability to distinguish between convincing and unconvincing evidence and arguments.

Finally, at AO2 you need to focus on rational argument, showing that you can:

- organise your points coherently
- display an understanding of theoretical debates in sociology
- marshall evidence to support your arguments and conclusions

Study skills and revision strategies

There are certain methods of studying that will help you specifically in sociology, and you will become familiar with these as you progress through your A2 course. The most basic skills, however, are central to your work in all subjects.

- Devise a consistent method of taking notes, both from your teachers and from your reading. Various techniques and forms of shorthand are available. Try some out, decide what works best for you, and stick to it.
- Review your notes at regular intervals.
- Produce reduced versions of your notes for later revision.
- Practise doing examination questions regularly.
- Read everything your teacher asks you to, and if possible add books or articles on aspects of a topic that particularly interest you.

- Keep to your teacher's homework timetable, handing in work when it is due and paying attention to comments and feedback.

The second set of study skills is more particularly relevant to A-level Sociology.

- Try to read a quality daily newspaper or at least a quality Sunday newspaper. Newspapers like the *Guardian*, *Observer*, *Independent* or *The Times* contain invaluable comment on a whole range of sociological topics. You can also practise applying your critical and evaluative skills to the news stories and memorise examples to use in your examination. Use your school or local library as a source of these newspapers.
- Try to get plenty of experience in using the internet. There are some excellent sites dedicated to A-level Sociology as well as more general sociological sites that are interesting and thought-provoking. The ATSS site at **www.atss.org.uk** is a good starting-point.
- Subscribe to *Sociology Review* and consult back copies held by your school or college library. It is one of the best sources of contemporary sociological work in the areas you will be examined on.
- Watch television and films from a sociological point of view and try to apply appropriate concepts to the stories. Discuss the programmes with your parents and siblings and see what they make of your analysis.

Where revision strategies are concerned, the following points are especially important:

- Before you start your revision, get yourself a copy of the awarding body's specification so that you know what you need to cover.
- Draw up a revision timetable covering the two months before the examination. Plan for all your subjects, making sure you allow yourself some free time. Be organised! On no account leave all your revision until the last few days. Get a good night's sleep before the exam.
- Revise actively — don't just sit there and read your notes. Try to do exercises and activities that test your AO2 skills.
- Practise 'real' exam questions as often as you can. Use the answers in this unit guide as exemplars that illustrate how you could improve your performance.
- Listen to your teachers and act on their advice and instructions. They are trying to help you, not make your life miserable.
- In the exam, divide your time according to the marks available for each section and make sure that you attempt all parts of each question you decide to answer.

The unit test

Religion is a Module 4 topic. This module also contains the topics of World Sociology and Power and Politics. In the unlikely event that you have covered more than one of these topics in your course, you will need to choose only one of the three sections on the examination paper (Religion is Section B). You must answer Part One of the question, which consists of questions 4(a) and 4(b). This is compulsory. In Part Two there are two questions and you must choose only one of these (question 5 or question 6). The whole section is worth 15% of the A-level qualification and is therefore an important component. As we have seen, 6% of the marks are given to AO1 and 9% to AO2. Unit 4 Section B questions are worth 60 marks in total, with 8 marks given to question 4(a), 12 marks to question 4(b) and 40 marks to either question 5 or question 6, depending upon which you choose.

Attached to Part One will be a single item of source material. Read this carefully before attempting to answer question 4(a) and/or (b). It may provide you with important information and clues for one or more of the parts. When one of the questions refers specifically to the source material ('Using Item A' or 'With reference to Item A and elsewhere'), you are *required* to make use of it. You should do this as obviously as possible, using phrases such as 'As Item A demonstrates...' or 'The view in Item A suggests that ...' so that the examiner can easily identify the points where you draw on the source material.

The number of marks available for the various elements you have to answer (8, 12 and 40) indicates the time that you should allocate to each element. As you have 1 hour and 30 minutes, you should devote roughly 60 minutes to question 5 or 6, about 15 minutes to question 4(b) and about 10 minutes to question 4(a), leaving 5 minutes for reading through and reviewing at the end. While the balance of AO1 and AO2 marks in questions 5 or 6 is equal (20 marks for AO1 and 20 marks for AO2), for questions 4(a) and 4(b) AO2 marks are in the majority. For 4(a) AO1 is given 0 marks and AO2 all 8 marks. For 4(b) AO1 is given 4 marks and AO2 8 marks. The most important thing to keep in mind is that examiners at A-level are looking for evidence that you have developed the skills of identification, analysis, interpretation and evaluation — take every opportunity to demonstrate them. Read the questions carefully for clues as to the particular skills you are expected to show. Having said all this, do not neglect to show evidence of knowledge and understanding of the material covered in the topic.

The range of issues that may be examined in this module are covered in the Content Guidance section.

Content Guidance

This section is intended to show you the major issues and themes covered in **Religion** and the main points of evaluation that have been made about them. We have also identified the key concepts and key writers in each area. You must remember, though, that these are offered as guidance only. It is always a good idea to read some original research in a particular area and religion is full of interesting and accessible books and articles. If these are not available to you, most of the textbooks for the course have good accounts of relevant ideas and arguments. Your teacher will also give you other studies during your course. The main magazine for A-level sociologists, *Sociology Review*, has repeatedly focused on issues in religion, so back copies, available from your school or college library, are a useful source of information.

The content of the topic falls into five main areas:
- **theories of religion**
- **the role of religion in society**
- **forms of religious organisation**
- **the relationship between religious beliefs, religious organisations and social groups**
- **the secularisation debate**

The AQA A2 specification is designed to give you a comprehensive understanding of the importance of these areas in contemporary and past societies. You will be expected to be familiar with the major sociological explanations of religion, in terms of its functions for society and for individuals. This includes the classical sociologists' views on religion, which were central to their understanding of the operation of societies, as well as more recent approaches such as postmodernism. You will also need to be familiar with the range of different religious organisations that exist and their relationship to various social groups. Lastly, one of the main debates in the sociology of religion is its continued importance in contemporary societies and the contradictory evidence about the development of a secular society. This debate occurs at three levels — society, religious practices and individual consciousness.

Theories of religion

Definitions

Key ideas

- Definitions are important because they decide what should be examined as a religious phenomenon and what should not.
- Inclusivist definitions include many phenomena that might seem controversial, such as magic, or even non-religious, such as communism.
- Exclusivist definitions exclude phenomena that do not make reference to a supernatural being and limit what can be defined as religious.
- Functional definitions of religion focus on the role that a religious phenomenon performs for society as a whole, such as acting as a unifying force.
- Substantive definitions refer to a defining characteristic, such as a belief in a transcendent God, as the distinctive feature of religion.
- Inclusivist definitions are 'essentialist', that is, they take the position that religious activity is a necessary feature of the human condition, although it may take many forms.
- Exclusivist definitions are 'non-essentialist', accepting that there may be a decline or growth in religious activity at different historical stages.
- The definition adopted leads the sociologist to ask different questions about the scale and importance of religious belief and activity in society, and possibly to reach different conclusions.

Evaluation

- + Inclusivist-functionalist definitions allow the sociologist to investigate a wide range of historical and contemporary practices as 'religious', including humanism and psychoanalysis, because these are concerned with the 'ultimate problems' that confront all human beings.
- + Exclusivist-substantive definitions allow the sociologist to examine only those social phenomena that are commonsensically recognised as expressions of religious feeling.
- + Both approaches are attempting to identify what can be 'religious' in order to form a field of study with definite boundaries.
- − Inclusivist-functional definitions are drawn so wide that they make the idea of a specifically religious sphere of activity difficult to maintain — everything can be seen as 'religious'.
- − Exclusivist-substantive definitions limit what can be seen as religious and lead inevitably to the idea that religious observance has declined in importance, as its manifestation changes in society.
- − Both approaches are actually linked to ideological positions that are associated with either supporting or undermining religious belief.

inclusivism, exclusivism, functionalism, essentialism, transcendence

Durkheim, Weber, Bellah, Yinger, Robertson

Durkheim

Key ideas

- Durkheim started from the position that social existence was only possible through the belief in shared ideas.
- He offered a functionalist definition of religion, as being 'beliefs and practices which unite into one single moral community called a Church'.
- Religion was therefore an essential part of the 'conscience collective', or the shared ideas that make social life possible.
- These shared ideas constituted the fundamental notions of time, space, causation and relationships that allow humankind to think logically.
- He distinguished between the 'profane' and the 'sacred', the former being everyday life and the latter constituting things set apart and forbidden.
- He drew these ideas from a study of the totemic religions of the Australian aborigines, in which the totem worshipped was usually a representation of the name of the clan.
- The totem also symbolised society and the collective rituals of religion. In this sense it was a restatement of the importance of social bonds.
- Religion therefore acted to bind individuals to society, allowing them to understand and enact correct social relations between individuals, through the shared values of religious belief.
- Religion also regulated behaviour so that social life became possible without selfish individualism getting in the way.

+ Durkheim offered a functional explanation in which religion is given a dominant role in social cohesion.
+ He identified a moral dimension to the nature of social relationships, based on religious ideas.
+ He explained the existence of religion in terms of its rituals rather than its theological ideas.
− Durkheim ignored the importance of individual religious experience, focusing on the structural elements of religion.
− He had a static view of religion; for example, he did not attempt to explain the rise of new religions or religious leaders.
− The practices of primitive religions do not explain the workings of religion in a complex, religiously diverse modern society.

Key concepts

conscience collective, sacred, profane, totems, representation

Key thinkers

Durkheim, Eister

Weber and Weberian approaches

Key ideas

- Weber believed that ideas, including religious ideas, had an independent effect on social and economic change.
- To demonstrate this, he examined the relationship between new religious ideas and the development of the capitalist system of production.
- Specifically he argued that the ethical orientation of Calvinist Protestants led to practices that gave impetus to capitalist modes of production — the 'spirit of capitalism'.
- Catholic culture was portrayed as being concerned with conspicuous consumption, whereas Protestantism encouraged a frugal frame of mind in which income was ploughed back into production rather than spent on luxuries.
- There was thus an 'elective affinity' between the Protestant ethic and the spirit of capitalism; the Protestant ethic was not the sole causal relationship, but an important factor.
- The ideas of Calvinism produced a particular personality trait that acted out patterns of conduct conducive to the development of capitalism.
- Weber also examined other religions to see if there were reasons why they did not lead to the development of capitalist modes of behaviour.
- Confucianism stressed adjustment to the world. By contrast, the uncertainty of Calvinism had the unintended consequence of leading believers to see worldly success as a sign of God's favour.
- Bellah argued that the relationship between religion and economics is indirect, operating through the political structure, rather than directly.
- Wertheim argued that all ideas have a transformative capacity, not just religious ones.

Evaluation

- \+ Weber stressed the importance of ideas as causal factors in social developments, rejecting economic determinism.
- \+ He sought to explain social change as a complex interplay of forces, but in which there are decisive points in history that can be identified through sociological analysis.
- \+ Weber's argument offers a cross-cultural approach to social change, using data from a number of societies to explore a particular hypothesis and come to a conclusion.

– Weber did not demonstrate how strongly individual entrepreneurs held their religious beliefs and therefore whether these affected their patterns of behaviour.

    – It has been claimed that the connection between religion and economics has been over-stressed, with many other factors suggested as the cause of capitalism.

    – It has been argued that it was not the religious belief of the Calvinists that was important for the development of capitalism but their marginal position in a Catholic society that led them to strive for wealth.

Key concepts

Calvinistic Protestantism, spirit of capitalism, elective affinity, transformative capacity, cross-culturalism

Key thinkers

Weber, Tawney, Wertheim, Sombart

Marx

Key ideas

- Marx saw religion as an aspect of ideology, rather than as important in its own right.
- It was an important element in the 'false consciousness' of the workers and of the bourgeoisie, in that neither had a real appreciation of their position as pawns of the system.
- For the workers, religion was one way in which their alienation was alleviated, focusing their attention on the rewards of the next world rather than the misery of this one.
- However, religion also represented the workers' yearning for a better world, their hopes for a future better than their present situation.
- For the bourgeoisie, religion was a cloak of respectability behind which they relentlessly pursued profit at the expense of the workers.
- Protestantism, with its emphasis on the 'abstract individual' facing his or her maker alone, allowed the bourgeoisie to treat their workers not as men or women but as commodities to be bought and sold.
- Both bourgeoisie and proletariat were subject to the impersonal forces of capitalism, which destroyed and favoured individuals in an apparently random fashion for which no religion could compensate.
- Kautsky argued that it was the development of capitalism that led to the creation of Protestant ideas, to justify the economic activities of the bourgeoisie.

Evaluation

+ The phenomenon of religion is seen by Marxism as being determined by the economic base, so giving primary importance to economic activity rather than ideas.

+ The positions of both proletariat and bourgeoisie are explained in terms of the role of religion in an inhumane system.

+ Religion is seen as a delusion of the mind, designed to accommodate individuals to their lot.

− Marxism dismisses the reality of sincere religious feelings that individuals experience.

− It is monocausal, explaining religion purely as an epiphenomenon of the economic system.

− Religion has an impact on social groups other than just social classes, such as ethnic groups, but these are not addressed.

Key concepts

alienation, bourgeoisie, proletariat, false consciousness

Key thinkers

Feuerbach, Marx, Kautsky

Functionalism

Key ideas

- Though drawn from Durkheim, functionalist thought on religion differs from Durkheim's views in certain crucial respects.
- Totemism is not a set of unified practices, as envisaged by Durkheim, but ranges from very complex formulations to trivial phenomena like totem poles.
- Totemism can also be seen not as the relation of the individual to the social world, but as expressing the individual's relationship to the natural world (Levi-Strauss).
- An alternative functionalist theory was put forward by Malinowski, who saw religion as the response of individuals to the uncertainty of the world, fulfilling an emotional need for security.
- Religion can function to bind individuals together in the face of the death of one member of a group, through the comfort of collective rituals.
- Religion therefore makes a unique contribution to social integration.
- Any decline in religious belief or practice leads to increased social disorganisation.
- Religion, therefore, is an essential feature of all successful societies.
- It is the only aspect of human experience that can grasp the non-empirical, and as such is a necessary basis for human action.

Evaluation

+ Functionalism insists on looking at the social dimension rather than the individual for an explanation of religion.

+ By emphasising the importance of religion in social integration, it answers the Hobbesian 'problem of order' of how we can live together peacefully.

+ It attempts to deal with the supernatural as a 'real' phenomenon of subjective experience.

− Many societies seem to exist without a unifying religion in the conventional sense.

− Functionalism asserts rather than explains how religion reinforces common values, especially in multireligious societies.

- Religious participation/activity can exist without any corresponding strong religious belief.

Key concepts

totemism, social integration, the supernatural, social disorganisation

Key thinkers

Radcliffe-Brown, Levi-Strauss, Malinowski, Davis, Parsons

Interactionism

Key ideas

- Phenomenologists focus on the states of consciousness of individuals, including their religious consciousness, as they live out their everyday lives in the Lebenswelt.
- Religion is established by human enterprise or actions, in which objects or beings are given awesome power, standing apart from, but related to, the existence of humanity.
- This sacred dimension is the opposite of the chaos that confronts individuals as they try to make sense of their lives.
- Religion therefore gives us ultimate meanings, making the universe manageable by reducing it to a human-centred enterprise, in which we gain significance in the cosmic order.
- A higher plane of existence is indicated by many aspects of human experience — when we discover order in our lives, from the joy of play, from hope, from events experienced as evil, from humour.
- Religion is therefore about cognition, providing us all with the categories and concepts needed to make sense of the world.
- We all share these existential concerns (what is life, death, joy, suffering etc.) and all therefore have religiosity — a sense of the supernatural.
- As an individual phenomenon, contemporary religion has many of the features of a supermarket, in which individuals are free to choose or change according to personal inclination.

Evaluation

+ Interactionists take religious feeling and sensibility as a 'real' phenomenon experienced by people, rather than as a false consciousness.
+ Interactionism deals with the issue of 'ultimate meaning' rather than taking a strictly materialist approach.
+ It takes religion as an everyday activity rather than at the level of the institution.
− Interactionists place too much emphasis on the subjective meaning of religion, ignoring its power and influence on the institutional level, for example.
− Phenomenological approaches suffer from 'cognitive reductionism', over-emphasising the rational/thoughtful aspects of religion, against its emotional appeal.

content guidance

— Interactionism assumes that we all have a measure of religious feeling that must be fulfilled, when, in fact, religious sensibility can be shown to be distributed according to social class.

Key concepts

Lebenswelt, everyday world, spiritual supermarket, cognitive reductionism

Key thinkers

Berger, Berger and Luckmann, Turner, Bibby

Postmodernism

Key ideas

- With the collapse of religious certainty represented by the 'sacred canopy' of a universally accepted religion, individuals have to seek their own 'meaning-routes' through the wealth of religious choices on offer.
- As the old religious certainties fade, new forms of religious connectedness are made between individuals, either referring back to certainty or rejecting it in favour of the individual quest for truth.
- In a network society, where flows of power, wealth and information are beyond individual control, individuals may turn to the power of religious identity to try to exercise some control over their situation.
- As religion becomes 'à la carte', the choice is between forms of haute cuisine (traditional religion) and McDonaldisation (standardised but bland religious ideas).
- In a postmodern world of endless choice, religious fundamentalism is not a 'throw-back' but a rational response to 'choice overload', where the individual has to make myriad choices not only of consumer products, but also between ideas and values.
- The media are a crucial aspect of postmodern religion, with some sociologists seeing the internet as a new metaphor for the nature of God, being decentralised and dispersed (Turkle).
- As religion becomes packaged as a commodity in the market place, it becomes Disneyfied, that is, trivial and crowd-pleasing.
- Globalisation trends are reflected in the emergence of new religious movements that look for a unifying and common religious culture under such names as Gaia or planetary theology.

Evaluation

+ Postmodernism seeks to explain the explosion of religious sects and cults in contemporary capitalist societies.
+ It locates movements such as fundamentalism and planetary ecology within the conditions of contemporary postmodern living.
+ It emphasises the importance of the hyper-reality of the media in contemporary religious life.

- It overemphasises the degree to which the old certainties have collapsed and we are faced with genuine choices.
- Fundamentalism can be seen as a reactionary response to modernism, rather than a postmodern response to choice.
- Postmodernism denies the serious way in which individuals approach religion in favour of a 'playful' perspective.

Key concepts

network society, 'à la carte' religion, choice overload, McDonaldisation, Disneyfication

Key thinkers

Bauman, Castells, Limieux, Heelas, Turkle, Lyon

The role of religion

As a unifying force

Key ideas

- Where there is a 'sacred canopy' of a universal religion in a society, it can act as a force for solidarity.
- A common religion offers a set of values that shapes behaviour in a specific way, so that all are agreed on appropriate conduct.
- This can lead to a form of mechanistic solidarity in society, in which there is an identification through sameness, based on religious belief.
- Secular formations, such as the monarchy, use religious symbolism to reinforce their claim to represent the nation and act as a focus of loyalty.
- In a global society of mass migrations, religion can act as a unifying force for disparate populations; for example when an allegiance to Islam assists marginal populations to carve out an identity.
- The importance of Christianity in the United States is that it acts as a unifier of a mainly immigrant society, despite differences in the particular form of Christianity adopted.
- Diasporic populations, such as the Jews, use religion as a marker for identity, despite surface differences between forms of the religion, such as Orthodox or liberal or reform Judaism.
- In divided societies, such as Ireland, religion can act as a signifier, uniting distinct populations in opposition to the 'Other'.

Evaluation

+ This view emphasises the positive aspects of religion, showing it as a force for integration, identity and solidarity.

+ It explains the persistence of religious differences in populations characterised by migration.
+ It focuses on the common elements that members of a religion share, through an acceptance of shared ideas and allegiances.
− The idea of a unifying religious force is more appropriate for historical societies than for contemporary ones.
− The 'sacred canopy' idea overestimates the degree of real loyalty to and belief in an overarching religion, such as Catholicism in medieval Europe, as individuals often only pay lip-service to such beliefs.
− The history of religion suggests that it is more significant for its ability to divide people than unite them, as in religious wars or the contemporary Middle East.

Key concepts

integration, sacred canopy, diaspora, global society

Key thinkers

Durkheim, Shils, Parsons, Bellah

As a source of conflict

Key ideas

- Strong faith in a particular religion often involves a deep belief in the 'wrongness' of other religious forms, expressed in such terms as heresy, abomination and false belief.
- As a component of identity, religion can generate strong collective feelings that function to separate out often minority groups from mainstream society, so that conflict occurs over the allocation of resources to particular religious segments of the community.
- Religious allegiance often parallels other social divisions, particularly of class and ethnicity, compounding the potential for misunderstanding and conflict.
- Many religious faiths have a powerful 'missionary' zeal associated with them, in which adherents are called upon to proselytise (convert) the non-believer, by force if necessary.
- Historically and in contemporary politics, many wars have been and are fought in the name of religion; for example, the conflict in the Middle East and the 'war against terrorism' have a religious dimension to them.
- Where religions have an eschatological dimension (a belief in the end of the world), believers may be careless of their own earthly lives and strive for immortality through violent actions against those they identify as the enemy of their religion.
- Marxists claim that religious conflicts mask economic conflicts and therefore act as a smokescreen for the exploitation of the have-nots by the haves.
- Where there is a strong 'state' religion, in which one form of religious belief is given privileges by the state over all others, members of other religions may suffer

discrimination or disadvantage; for example, in Great Britain a Roman Catholic cannot legally become the monarch.

- Religion is often mixed up with political and cultural struggles over what is correct behaviour and beliefs for individuals, as evidenced in the fatwa against Salman Rushdie.

Evaluation

+ This view focuses on the history of religions rather than the content of their theology or ideology.
+ It suggests that religions have a 'dark side' and are not all peace and love to humankind.
+ It directs attention to the consequences of religious discrimination and the disadvantages that members of particular faiths may experience in society.
− It downplays the real good that religions have achieved in the world, in terms of both religious organisations and individual believers.
− It assumes that adherents to different religions are inevitably drawn into conflict through their religious differences.
− It ignores movements, such as ecumenicalism, that seek to forge bridges not just within different sections of the same world religions, but between members of all faiths.

Key concepts

fundamentalism, religion as a smokescreen, exclusivist religion

Key thinkers

Marx, Kepel, Wallis, Bromley and Shupe

As a conservative force

Key ideas

- The notion of religion as a conservative force is based on the links between the state and a specific religion in many societies, in which there are pervasive political, social and economic links between high-ranking members of the religion and political personalities.
- It is related to functionalist ideas that religion serves to integrate individuals into a dominant status quo, but goes further in arguing that religion seeks to defend political and social arrangements as they are.
- Religion thus has an important legitimising function for many regimes. For example, some claim that Methodism, because of its conservative nature, was one of the main reasons why the working classes did not revolt in nineteenth-century Britain.
- The classic example of the fusion of religious and political power is in the Vatican State, where the Papacy is both a temporal and a spiritual phenomenon.
- The involvement of Evangelical Christians in right-wing politics in the United States is seen as one of main manifestations of contemporary religious conservatism.

- This identification of religion with the status quo has led in some instances to the dominant religion of a society being associated with authoritarian and occasionally violent political regimes, such as in the case of Pinochet's Chile.
- The Iranian revolution of Ayatollah Khomenei can be seen either as a conservative revolution in defence of traditional Islamic values or as a reactionary movement against the modernisation and Westernisation of Iran by the Shah.
- There is also a wider sense in which religion can be seen as a conservative force, in that many long-established religions act in defence of 'traditional' values and ways of behaving and are often critical of modernising tendencies, such as Taliban rule in Afghanistan.
- The traditional conservative values of many religions seem to conflict with modern and postmodern ways of living, but are also powerful attractions to many individuals who are bemused by the complexities and lack of certainty in their lives.
- Many individuals are able to adhere to the conservative message of their religious beliefs while acting in ways that are contrary to them, for example many Roman Catholics practise birth control which is barred by the Catholic church.

Evaluation

+ This view places an emphasis on tradition and continuity that has a wide appeal in conditions of change.
+ It locates allegiance to a particular state in a religious context, thus legitimising and securing it against discontent and rebellion.
+ It identifies values that seem to have endured for many years and act as a call to 'correct behaviour'.
− The conservative leanings of many religious personalities have led to their defence of some unpleasant regimes that have little respect for human rights.
− Unquestioning support for the way things have always been impedes progress in many spheres of social life, for example in women's rights.
− Values that are unchanging are likely to conflict with changing social conditions and lead to misery for individuals as they juggle their beliefs and their way of life.

Key concepts

universal church, religious reaction, legitimation, anti-modernity, Westernisation

Key thinkers

Parsons, Troeltsch, Yinger, Halevy

As a source of change

Key ideas

- Drawn from the work of Weber, this approach emphasises the role of religion in stimulating social, political or economic change through the evolution of new religious ideas.

- It is associated with the thesis of the 'spirit of capitalism', in which the emergence of Calvinism acted as a spur to the development of capitalist modes of behaviour that transformed feudal societies.
- This view of religions is based on the idea that they contain within them the potential for both reactionary and radical actions, and therefore religious believers can be mobilised for progressive causes.
- Liberation theology of the 1960s and 1970s is seen as an example of the 'commitment to the poor' by worker-priests in Latin America, which led many grass-root leaders of the Roman Catholic church to involve themselves in radical and even revolutionary movements.
- With an emphasis on justice and fairness, many religious movements, such as the World Council of Churches, supported the anti-apartheid movement in South Africa.
- Where religion forms an oppositional focus to repressive regimes, it can be used as a vehicle for political change, even where it is violent, such as in the Iranian revolution.
- Religious organisations also formed the basis of many anti-colonial movements in Africa, such as Alice Lenshina's Church in Zambia, where the mix of Christian and traditional religious forms was an attempt to establish an authentic African voice.
- Religion also formed the core of resistance of native Americans to encroachment by white society during the period of the 'Ghost Dances' in the late nineteenth century.

Evaluation

+ This approach acknowledges the contradictory potential of religion for both conservative and radical ends.
+ It develops a historical perspective in understanding the nature of religion as a tool of the oppressed to resist their condition.
+ It offers a positive view of religion's role in society, stressing its potential for achieving essential changes needed to promote values, such as justice, which are both secular and religious.
− It tends to overestimate the success of religious movements in promoting social change, as in Latin America where liberation theology has been essentially neutralised.
− It sees social change as an end in its own right, without examining the consequences of such change for the people it is supposed to assist, for example justifying repressive regimes that might emerge as a result.
− It downplays other forces for social change in favour of religion, negating economic and political movements such as the anti-colonial movement.

Key concepts

mobilisation, commitment to the poor, liberation theology

Key thinkers

Weber, Wilson, Debray, Mooney

Religious organisations

Church and sect

Key ideas

- A fundamental distinction in Christian religious organisations is the difference between church and sect as elaborated by Troeltsch.
- Both churches and sects believe that only their members will gain salvation and that the adherents of other organisations or religions will not be in a 'state of grace'.
- Churches believe that salvation is given in a mystical manner as an infant is received through baptism into the pre-existing church ('salvation through grace'). The individual is therefore born into the church, experiencing it as an objective reality with a long tradition.
- Sects believe that salvation depends upon the rational assent of the adult individual to believe in a personal God and to live in a voluntary community of 'saints', made up of the other believers ('salvation through faith').
- Churches are positive in their attitudes towards the established social order, often having formal links with the state. In some cases their higher personnel are drawn from the upper classes.
- Sects are more associated with lower social classes, separate from the establishment, and have a more tense relationship with the state, sometimes being in strong opposition to the secular order.
- Churches develop ideologies to defend and legitimate the status quo, such as the divine right of kings in monarchical societies. These ideologies may become outdated as social circumstances change, but are retained as part of the tradition of the church.
- Sects tend not to look to the past but to live in the present, 'living the life' of faith, with their values constantly being renewed as a result of their everyday experiences of God's presence.
- Churches and sects should not be seen only in uniform terms, nor as resistant to change. Churches have within them enthusiastic and evangelical elements, while sects are subject to routinisation and also have a formal element.

Evaluation

+ This distinction identifies key respects in which religious organisations may differ.
+ It is a useful tool to use when beginning to analyse the behaviour and ideas of religious organisations.
+ It focuses on the social dimension of religious organisations, examining their relationship with social hierarchies.
− The distinction is more appropriate to an earlier period of history, when, during the Reformation, Europeans were divided between a Catholic church and oppositional Protestant sects.

– It does not take account of the dynamics of religious organisations, which can change their forms over time, with churches becoming more sect-like and vice versa.
– Sects are less persecuted in contemporary Western societies and may therefore have lost their antipathy to the state.

Key concepts

legitimation, opposition, salvation through grace, salvation through faith, routinisation

Key thinkers

Weber, Troeltsch, Barker

Denominations and cults

Key ideas

- Denominations were described by Niebuhr as 'a compromise between Christianity and the world' to indicate that they were distinctive from and somewhere between the formalism of churches and the inspirationalism of sects.
- Originally sect-like in their religious devotion, as the second generation was born they took on more of the attributes of churches.
- The crucial issue that turned some sects towards more routinised forms of worship was that of baptising infants. While sects emphasised adult baptism, some members wanted their children to be brought up in the organisation and used infant baptism as a sign of their commitment. This turned them to more church-like practices which came to be associated with denominations.
- The growing wealth of sect members as they lived frugal and productive lives in their faith eventually contributed to the development of many sects into more formal denominations.
- However, there was no inevitability in this process. Wealthy sects could retain their sect-like character or renew their enthusiasm rather than become routinised.
- Denominations are distinct from sects and churches in their non-universalist approach; that is, they accept that there are other ways to salvation than just through membership of their specific organisation.
- A further complication of the typology of religious organisations is the existence of cults.
- Cults were originally a private form of religion, usually with a mystic dimension.
- 'Cult' is widely used now to indicate secretive and domineering sect-like organisations that may operate with manipulative mind-control techniques and have a highly exclusivist agenda, cutting off adherents from family non-believers.
- Wallis classifies churches, sects, denominations and cults according to whether the wider world sees them as being respectable (church and denomination) or deviant (sects and cults), as well as whether they see themselves as being the only road to salvation (church and sect) or not (denomination and cult).

Evaluation

+ These categories add to our understanding of the complexity of types of religious organisation.
+ They emphasise processes of change in the form of religious organisations and stress the importance of social development in the evolution of any specific organisation.
+ The concept of the 'cult' allows an exploration of some of the more negative aspects of religious organisations.
− Not all sects believe in the values of thrift. Therefore, there is no necessary process of becoming wealthy and upwardly mobile, thus creating the impetus towards a denomination.
− Many sects, for example the Jehovah's Witnesses, far from being led by charismatic and inspirational leaders, are very bureaucratic, so routinisation cannot be claimed as a feature of becoming a denomination.
− The idea of the cult creates a stereotype of religious organisations that can be used to criticise the activities of any of them.

Key concepts

formalism, inspirationalism, baptism, non-universalism, mysticism

Key thinkers

Niebuhr, von Weise, Wallis

More complex views of religious organisation

Key ideas

- The range of religious organisations is much larger than the four-fold divisions of church, sect, denomination and cult suggested by many typologies.
- In addition, the role of any religious organisation cannot be said to be either conservative or radical at all times, but varies according to which level of the organisation is examined, the cultural context within which it operates, as well as the nature of its beliefs.
- 'Universal church' refers to a dominant religious form that is cross-national and operates independently of individual political units. An example is Roman Catholicism before the Reformation.
- An ecclesia refers to a religion that is identifiable as the state religion of a specific nation-state, such as Shia Islam in Iran.
- An established sect refers to a long-lived sect that has made an accommodation with the state over most issues, but remains opposed to the state on certain specifics. The pacifism of the Quaker movement is an example.

- Sects can take many forms and can be classified according to their attitude towards the secular world. They may accept it as a something to be lived with and celebrated, or avoid the world completely, or be actively opposed and hostile to the secular powers.
- Sects can be further divided into many different types, from the conversionist, evangelical, fundamentalist sects to thaumaturgical sects which seek contact with a spirit world.
- The relationship of any religious organisation to the world is therefore complex, and each empirical example needs to be examined separately rather than stereo-typically.

Evaluation

+ These complex typologies offer a more complete understanding of the nature of religious organisations.
+ They put forward a more dynamic view of the way that religious organisations operate in the world.
+ They suggest that religious organisations are subject to processes of change, as well as rooted in tradition.
− All these typologies can be criticised for focusing mainly on Christian organisa-tions and ignoring or downplaying the other major world religions.
− Complex typologies can become so convoluted that they cease to have any explanatory power.
− The examples used to support particular typologies can often be based on a stereotypical view of the real religious life of organisations.

Key concepts
universal church, ecclesia, established sect, acceptance, opposition

Key thinkers
Yinger, Wilson, Maguire

New Religious Movements

Key ideas

- 'New Religious Movements' is a term used to describe the many forms of religious groups that have emerged throughout the world, separate from the traditional forms of world religions, but often related to them.
- World-rejecting NRMs, such as Krishna Consciousness, are inward-looking and strict organisations that tend to avoid contact with outsiders as far as possible, in the search for spiritual enlightenment.
- World-affirming NRMs, such as Scientology, see success in the secular world as one of the aims of their spiritual journey within it.
- World-accommodating NRMs, such as Neo-Pentecostalism, are outward-looking, tolerant and charismatic movements.

- Some NRMs are accused of using brain-washing techniques and isolation of members from their families as a means of control, and can be associated with the absolute dominance of a charismatic leader, at whose command members will even take their own life.
- NRMs are believed to emerge during times of social change and are often seen as perfect for the postmodern era with its loss of certainty, in offering those in search of answers a 'true' account of the world.
- NRMs are said to offer recruits success in careers, improved health and self-development and 'authentic' religious experience.
- NRMs are often difficult to leave, partly because of the psychological investment that has been made in them, but also because the usual social ties may have been cut and continuing members may be hostile to the leaver.
- There has been much media attention on the 'doomsday' NRMs, whose members have engaged in acts either of suicide (Jonesville) or of terror (Aum Shinrikyo).
- A particular form of NRM is the political coalition of fundamentalist Christian groups in the United States (New Christian Right), which seek to impose their beliefs on the rest of society by influencing the president. They have gained a significant measure of political influence in President Bush's administration.
- New Age Movements, such as paganism, Gaia and astrology, are also seen as a form of alternative NRM, with a focus on inner spirituality, the environment, and forms of spiritualism and Eastern mysticism.

Evaluation

+ 'New Religious Movement', as a wider term than sect or cult, is a more appropriate way of defining the many religious groups that emerged in the latter part of the twentieth century.
+ NRMs have introduced a revival of religious feeling and devotion in many societies, and have attracted those who might otherwise be turned off from mainstream religion.
+ NRMs have had a positive effect on the mainstream Christian church in introducing charismatic behaviour and worship into traditional congregations.
− There is wide variation in NRMs, and many do not fit easily into the various categories proposed, nor do they emerge only in times of instability.
− NRMs are stereotyped as being 'dangerous' and controlling, when they may offer members reassurance and control over their own lives.
− NRMs are nothing new, as there have always been subterranean religious forms. However, in the past they were more likely to be criticised or even suppressed for being heretical.

Key concepts

world-affirming, world-rejecting, world-accommodating, charismatic, New Age, New Christian Right

Key thinkers

Wallis, Barker, Beckford, Davie

Religion and social groups

Religion and class

Key ideas

- From a Marxist perspective, religion has been seen as functioning as an ideology in defence of the interests of the dominant social class in society.
- Interest theorists argue that religious ideas are a weapon in the struggle for advantage between different social groups and as a mask for real social and economic conflicts. Membership of specific religious organisations acts to further an individual's social and economic interests and marginalises those who do not belong.
- Strain theorists argue that religions emerge as a result of social dislocation and personal tensions and function to resolve these tensions (catharsis) in ways that are advantageous to those who adhere to them, from providing a scapegoat for unpleasant events in symbolic evil to legitimating strain in terms of a higher being. The strains that may be resolved by religion are not only economic, but also social (in terms of lack of power or esteem), organismic (mental or physical impairment), psychic (anomie) and ethical (dissatisfaction with society's values).
- At the base of these theories is the fact that different social classes profess allegiance to different forms of religion, even within a broad world religion; for example, Shia Islam draws recruits mainly from among the poorer sections of Afghanistan.
- In Great Britain, the Church of England has been dominated by a middle-class membership as the Anglican church has failed to recruit among the urbanised working classes.
- Some Protestant denominations, as well as Islam, Sikhism and Hinduism, find strong support in the working classes.
- Sects are sometimes seen as recruiting mainly from the disadvantaged in society, offering solutions to the pressures such people experience.
- Central to the appeal of religions are their 'theodices of good and ill fortune' — explanations for suffering or success that legitimate the position of those who experience either.
- Religion therefore acts as a 'compensator', offering rewards in the future, either on earth or in some form of heaven, for living a 'good life' here and now.

Evaluation

+ There is a class basis for many religious organisations and this has been explained through concepts such as compensators.
+ There is a link between world-affirming sects and the advantaged in society, and world-rejecting sects and the poor. This shows the importance of exploring the class nature of NRMs.

+ There are strong religious feelings among all social classes that express themselves in different ways and in different organisations.
− Sects are not just havens for the poor and dissatisfied, but also recruit from the rich and those who seemingly have everything.
− The statistical link between class and different types of sect is uncertain, especially because there are so few members of sects and cults.
− The appeal of religion is not universal among social classes and most individuals do not formally align to any religious organisation in contemporary Britain.

Key concepts

ideology, catharsis, solidarity, compensators

Key thinkers

Geertz, Glock and Stark, Stark and Bainbridge, Wallis

Religion and gender

Key ideas

- Many ancient religions had strong female images in the form of goddesses, but these have mainly been supplanted by male-dominated monotheistic religions such as Judaism, Christianity and Islam.
- The major religions therefore tend to privilege maleness in their theology, beliefs and practices.
- Where women are represented in religious beliefs, they tend to be in a submissive role or as agents of evil or temptation.
- Religious organisations are mainly male-led, with the position of priest being barred to females in some major religions.
- Where females are allowed to take positions of authority or sacramental roles, it is only after long and protracted struggles by female (and male) adherents to open up such positions (as was seen in the bitter opposition among some members of the Anglican church to the ordination of women).
- Many religions seek to restrict the behaviour of women, emphasising modesty and submission to male authority. This can have a physical expression in the separation of male and female worshippers during religious services.
- Religions are often hostile to overt sexuality in women and seek to suppress the female libido.
- Debates over the role of women in religion are seen as an argument between 'modernisers' and 'traditionalists', with the former often accused of being secular contaminators of 'pure' forms of religion.
- Outward religious forms for women are often presented in Western societies as symbolic of the 'Other', for example the wearing of the veil (hijab) by Muslim women.
- Yet, in many religions, women form the majority of regular attenders at services.

+ In patriarchal societies the different roles for men and women within religion are often explained as suiting their different natures and therefore being 'natural'.
+ Belief in these differences has been strongly held by many ordinary members of various faiths over a long period of time.
+ According to many believers, the tradition of male domination that goes back to the founders of the major religions should be followed, as it is a result of divine instruction.
− Many women willingly accept the subordinate role that religion requires them to play, seeing obedience to the gender hierarchy as a God-given duty for womenkind.
− Many religions have 'liberal' strands within them that stress equality between the genders in the eyes of God.
− Women are increasingly making inroads into strongholds of male religious authority; for example, the acceptance of female priests in the Church of England.

Key concepts

patriarchy, monotheism, sexuality, ordination of women

Key thinkers

El Saadawi, McGuire, Barker, Aldridge

Religion and ethnic identity

Key ideas

- 'Identity' has three components: the knowledge that one belongs to a group; the positive or negative values of belonging to a group; and the emotional attachment to a group or distance from other groups.
- Religious identity is therefore the knowledge, values and feelings relating to membership of a religious minority or majority in a society.
- Religion is one of the basic building blocks of ethnic identity, alongside nationality, shared history, language and assumptions about the 'body' (for example genetic inheritance).
- Ethnic identities are multidimensional and also interpenetrative. For example, British Muslims have a shared identity across these dimensions, with a national identity as British citizens, values relating to membership of a British Muslim community and perhaps feelings of belonging to a global Ummah (community of believers).
- Religion provides individuals with many 'markers' of identity, such as customs, dress, food, rituals, celebrations etc., but these are often fluid rather than rigid, for example fusion cuisine.
- Religion may also prove a powerful marker of ethnic identity because it can be a means of dealing with 'bafflement', allowing minorities to make sense of their position in society and of discrimination that they may experience.

- In postmodern societies, the fluidity of social relations and the lack of a solid identity in an urban landscape infused with myriad cultures can lead to a turning back to religion as a source of community — the formation of 'neo-tribes'.
- Postmodern uncertainties of identity affect majorities as well as minorities, and Christian as well as non-Christian religious expression.

Evaluation

+ This approach locates religious identity within a set of other sources of identity, but shows the importance of religious belief for marginalised groups in society.
+ It offers a dynamic and open view of identity as not fixed in a traditional formation but as adaptive to the realities of postmodern living.
+ It helps to explain the persistence of religious attachment amongst certain sections of the population within a generally more secular society.
− Some versions of identity theory fall into 'primordialism', that is, they argue that ethnic communities are 'natural' and exclusivist.
− Identity theory can overemphasise the attachment of young members of ethnic minorities in particular to religious belief, rather than the forms of religious behaviour, as a marker of identity.
− It can assume that ethnic majorities are more secular than ethnic minorities because of their majority position, which means they take their identity for granted.

Key concepts

social identity, Ummah, primordialism, neo-tribes

Key thinkers

Tafjel, Nash, Geertz, Berger, Bauman

Religion and fundamentalism

Key ideas

- Fundamentalism is the strict assertion of the basic beliefs of a religion, often expressed as a belief in the literal truth of the holy book of a religion.
- It can be seen more broadly as a conservative interpretation of faith, in which there is an emphasis on traditional values while the techniques of modernity are accepted as a means of spreading the conservative message.
- Fundamentalism can also be seen as a response by religious individuals and groups to the uncertainties of the postmodern world, with an emphasis on leading life according to the truth as revealed by God.
- While using modern techniques of propaganda, fundamentalism is a profound rejection of modernity and seeks to impose its vision of a holy state on the whole of society.
- It is expressed in different ways in different religions, from the traditional dress of Ultra-Orthodox Jews, who reject the Israeli state, to the jihadis of the Taliban who

controlled Afghanistan until 2002, and the New Christian Right political movement in the United States.

- Certain issues become talismanic for fundamentalist beliefs, such as opposition to abortion for some Christians or the wearing of the chador for women under strict Islamic rules.
- What unites all fundamentalists is their dislike of secularism and the liberal consensus of the Western world, which they view as responsible for disorder, crime and sinfulness.
- Education is often a key battleground for fundamentalist groups, whether it concerns the teaching of creationism by the Christian Right or the right of Islamic women to wear the veil in undenominational French schools. The growth of fundamentalist schools is becoming an important political issue.
- In Islam, the growth of fundamentalist belief is associated with the domination of the West over the Muslim world and an anti-Americanism which sees the United States as the 'Great Satan'.

Evaluation

+ Fundamentalism represents an authentic religious response through recalling an era of true religiosity.
+ The growth of fundamentalist organisations has been prolific and can perhaps be explained as a reaction against postmodernity, in which all metanarratives have been undermined.
+ The events of 11 September 2001 illustrate the magnitude of the challenge fundamentalism may pose to an allegedly 'corrupt' and 'degenerate' West.
− Fundamentalism was born out of the Christian religion and is not easily translated to the other world religions, especially Islam, where the Qur'an is seen as literally the word of God by all Muslims.
− It is uncertain how far fundamentalism has actually grown. As the most vocal of religious groups, fundamentalists tend to dominate religious discourse and drown out the voice of the moderate religious majority.
− Different societies have various responses to the perceived growth of fundamentalism, from political accommodation (United States under the Republicans) to opposition (Algeria).

Key concepts

literalism, laïcité, talismanic

Key thinkers

Kepel, Bruce, Modood

Secularisation

What is secularisation?

Key ideas

- An overarching definition of secularisation might be 'the loss of influence of religion over society and over individuals'.
- Secularists believe that there is a logic to history that leads people and societies increasingly to reject religious forms and instead embrace non-religious ideas and behaviours.
- Many early theorists were hostile to religion and saw its decline as inevitable as reason and science 'explained' religious 'myths'.
- The rationalisation of society, according to Weber, means that people put aside tradition and charisma in favour of reason and science.
- The quantum theory of religion suggests that part of human nature is an innate religiosity, which means that religious forms or expressions may change, but religion in one form or another is always with us.
- The definition of religion affects whether secularisation can be said to have happened or not. Exclusivist definitions tend to involve secularisation as 'pure' forms of religion evolve to respond to social changes. Inclusivist definitions, meanwhile, assume that there will always be some form of religion in society as it is essential for the maintenance of good relationships between members.
- Shiner argues that secularisation has been used by sociologists in at least six different ways, employing as many definitions.

Evaluation

- + Without the concept of secularisation, it would be difficult to examine social change in religious habits and beliefs.
- + The definition of secularisation is an important issue because it determines the way that sociologists try to measure it.
- + It is vital to know exactly what is being studied so that sociologists can explore the phenomenon rigorously.
- − Definitions can cut off areas of exploration as well as open them up.
- − Definitions of secularisation are predicated on pre-existing beliefs about the importance of religion. Those who see religion as essential do not accept that secularisation has occurred at all.
- − There have been many sociological studies focusing on how to define secularisation rather than exploring the empirical reality of religious behaviour.

Key concepts

secularisation, charisma, rationalisation, science

Key thinkers

Weber, Wilson, Shiner, Robertson, Beckford

Secularisation and society

Key ideas

- The basic notion in looking at society and religion is drawn from Wilson's view that religion 'loses its social significance'.
- This implies that previously well-accepted religious symbols and institutions become less important and lose their status in society.
- This can occur in several ways, such as atrophy or bureaucratisation or the loss of religious thought as a guide to action.
- The process began with the Reformation, which introduced choice into religious belief from the unitary world of medieval Catholicism. Choice reduces religion to servicing the needs of distinctive interest groups rather than embodying a whole society.
- The process is called societalisation and is where personal ties are replaced by contractual bonds between individuals, such that the role of the priest as a personal advocate for the individual with God is lost.
- Secular societies welcome social change, while religious societies are resistant. It is therefore the cities, the forges of change, that are the centre of the de-Christianisation of society.
- Religion therefore retreats into the private sphere and loses its public prominence, although vestiges may remain, such as the position of the bishops of the Church of England in the House of Lords.
- This process involves a loss of social status for the clergy and a reduction in the economic power of the church, with a subsequent decline in the proportion of the GDP that is spent on spiritual matters.
- The roles performed by the church are also depleted as societies industrialise and specialised secular agencies emerge to carry out functions originally performed by the church, such as ministering to the poor.
- This loss of functions for the church is accompanied by a shift among the churches to a 'this-worldly' orientation, using advertising techniques to attract adherents and forming unions among small denominations to combat declining attendance.
- Ecumenicalism is therefore a sign of structural weakness rather than a revival of true religious feeling.

Evaluation

- + There has clearly been some decline in the power of the church to influence social policies and historical events in Western societies.
- + Structural differentiation is a feature of modernisation and inevitably involves some loss of functions for religious institutions.
- + The economic and social decline of religious institutions has a physical manifestation in the deconsecration and sale of redundant churches.
- − This theory presupposes a 'golden age of religion' in which there was one dominant religious organisation. Even at the height of Catholic domination of

Europe, the church was riven by disputes, heretical movements and subterranean theologies.

– There is a difference between attendance at church for social reasons and for the purpose of worship. It may be that there never was any golden age of belief from which a decline has occurred.

– The extent to which formal religious institutions have lost power varies from society to society and it may be a Western phenomenon, not paralleled, for example, in Islamic societies.

Key concepts

atrophy, bureaucratisation, societalisation, loss of functions, structural differentiation

Key thinkers

Wilson, Shiner, Berger, Parsons

Religious practices

Key ideas

- At the level of culture, it is argued that there has been a shift of beliefs and behaviour away from a religious or spiritual frame of reference towards a secular frame.
- An example of this shift is the emergence of 'secular' or 'civil' religions, where there are outward signs of religious behaviour but in relation to secular objects. The ideology of Marxism is often cited as an example, with its 'saints', 'icons' and metaphysical belief in a better world.
- These secular beliefs are functional equivalents of religion in a postmodern world and constitute a surrogate religiosity.
- There is also a decline in the observance of religious forms, as measured in a number of ways:
  - There is a drop in the formal membership of the major churches, which is not offset by a rise in those who belong to the more marginal religious groupings.
  - The church is used less frequently for rites of passage such as baptism, marriage and funerals, with the latter still being the most 'popular' use of the church's facilities.
  - There is a fall in the number of people who attend church on either a regular or an occasional basis.
  - Regular Sunday attendance has dropped, as has observance of major festivals such as Christmas, which are more secular than ever before.
  - The growth in alternative forms of entertainment such as television has led to a fall off in, for example, Sunday school attendance.
- There has been a growth in religious pluralism which has altered the way that individuals practise their beliefs. For example, the growing House Church movement stands outside the traditional churches and is not taken into account in the official statistics for attendance.

- However, the element of choice implicit in religious pluralism suggests a fragmentation of religious behaviour and the potential for individuals to move between religious institutions during their life course.
- Many sects with growing membership are said to be only superficially religious and to function more as religious surrogates, being aimed at secular success rather than representing a return to real religiosity.

Evaluation

+ There is a consistent trend, year on year, towards fewer instances of religious observance, however measured.
+ Rituals and symbols need not have a religious dimension, but may fulfil a human need for pageantry and spectacle rather than a fundamental religiosity.
+ The shift towards secular forms of rites of passage is significant and is reflected in changing legislation, for example that which allows the performance of the marriage ceremony in any location.
− The issue of American exceptionalism is important here. The decline in religious observance has not occurred to the same extent in the United States as in Europe. This undermines claims for a general global secularisation.
− There is relatively little decline in the numbers who claim some affiliation to the major religions, and an increase in the numbers who align with sectarian and other forms of religious behaviour.
− There are methodological problems with collecting statistics on attendance and belief that make such statistics suspect and inconclusive.

Key concepts

secular religions, surrogate religiosity, exceptionalism

Key thinkers

Robertson, Bellah, Wilson

Religious consciousness

Key ideas

- Modernity has been characterised by a growth in rationality and the disenchantment of the world. This involves individuals discarding myth, charm and poetry to embrace scientific explanations.
- There has been a decline in belief in magic and superstition as natural phenomena become subject to scientific scrutiny. Magic is transformed into a theatrical event and superstitions become peripheral to everyday life.
- The ideology of science has permeated the consciousness of individuals and set up oppositions to irrational beliefs.
- One response of the religious community has been the growth of 'rational' religions that seek to reconcile scientificity with a belief in God. Rational religion is often counterposed to the growth of fundamentalist thinking.

- As the community of believers becomes smaller under the impact of industrialisation, the plausibility structure of religious belief (the institutions and networks that make belief in the irrational possible) is threatened.
- Surveys still show a high proportion of the population who profess a belief in a supernatural being, although the nature of the transcendental being is not always in accordance with traditional religious beliefs.
- Knowledge of orthodox religious doctrine is low, as is familiarity with the major text(s) of the religion to which people express an affiliation.
- It is claimed that religious ideas about morality have less of a hold over people's ideas and behaviour as they adopt secular alternatives.
- This is often manifested in the disjunction between the teachings of the church and the behaviour of those who claim strong allegiance to it, for example over birth control.

Evaluation

- + The growth in crime and anti-social behaviour is claimed to be the result of the loss of influence of religious morality over individual behaviour.
- + The unpopularity of religious education in schools and the decline in Sunday school attendance result in a lack of exposure to religious ideas among children.
- + Religious festivals, such as Christmas, are increasingly used as secular holidays rather than events imbued with religious meaning.
- – Scientific belief-systems cannot provide answers to ultimate questions and thus there will always be a search for the deeper reasons for existence.
- – There is still a large reservoir of belief in the subterranean theologies of magic and superstition, as demonstrated by the belief in astrology etc.
- – Polling information suggests that the impact of religion on individual consciousness may have decreased, but it still has a strong pull on people's consciences.

Key concepts

disenchantment, plausibility structure, Gods of the Gaps

Key thinkers

Berger, Wilson, Shiner

Anti-secularisation

Key ideas

- Secularisation theory is accused of being based on a teleological assumption; that is, it is a product of a Marxist/rationalist ideology which holds that, as societies modernise, they will get rid of old-fashioned ideas such as religion.
- Secularisation is therefore built on the back of a simplified view of history as a set of dualisms, in which religious/secular is affixed to traditional/modern.
- Rather than being an objective view of the development of societies, secularism represents an ideology that is unremitting in its hostility to all religious forms.

- Secularisation underestimates the diversity of different patterns of religious behaviour and thought under the conditions of modernity and postmodernity.
- Moreover, it is an ethnocentric view of religious developments, dismissing the persistence of religion in less economically developed countries as a result of their lack of modernity.
- Even in its own terms, secularisation theory does not hold true, as evidenced by the power of religious organisations in contemporary American society and the growth in sects.
- Rather than a decline in religion, society is seeing the growth of a 'new voluntarism' in religion, in which people have choices to make in a self-conscious reflexive process that might result in individuals continuing in the faith of their birth or joining a new form.
- Rational choice theory suggests that humans will always seek out a meaning to life and they make their religious choices by balancing the costs and benefits of adopting a particular belief system.
- In this sense we are religious consumers, calculating the cost of being committed to a particular set of rules and activities and setting this against the promised benefit of redemption.
- Our choices are made on the basis of different forms of religious commitment: the communal (to a community of believers), the ethical (to a belief-system), the cultural (to texts and traditions) and the emotional (to intensity of expression).

Evaluation

+ There is no inevitable decline in religion, rather religious observance varies across time and space and form.
+ The growth of non-standard religious institutions, such as fundamentalist sects, suggests that a religious revival is occurring, negating the secularisation thesis.
+ The development of rational choice theory offers an alternative way of explaining the empirical developments that have taken place.
− The emergence of new religious forms and the need to choose between them can be seen as a fragmentation of religion into a weakened and marginalised set of institutions.
− Secularisation theory is not just concerned with a dualistic view of history, but attempts to explain a complex and multifaceted phenomenon.
− It is difficult to apply the concept of rational individual choice to such an irrational form as religion.

Key concepts

consumerism, rational choice, religious commitment

Key thinkers

Martin, Wilson, Herberg, Bruce, Stark and Bainbridge, Hervieu-Léger

Questions & Answers

This section of the guide provides you with five questions on the topic of Religion in the style of the AQA unit test. The first four questions are followed by a grade-A response and a grade-C response. It is important to note that the grade-A answers are not model answers — they do not represent the only, or even necessarily the best, way of answering these questions. It would be quite possible, particularly in the answers to (b) and (c) questions, to take a different approach, or to use different material, or even to come to a different conclusion, and still gain high marks. The answers represent one way of answering the set question, bringing in suitable and relevant knowledge, showing good understanding, using appropriate theories, concepts and studies, displaying the necessary skills, particularly those of analysis and evaluation, and presenting a logically-structured argument. These four questions also have a grade-C candidate answer — one that is basically on the right track, but which fails, for various reasons, to score very high marks.

The fifth question is not accompanied by a student answer. This is for you to try on your own, though some guidance is given to help you.

Examiner's comments

The candidates' answers are interspersed with examiner's comments, preceded by the icon *e*. These comments identify why marks have been given and where improvements might be made, especially in the grade-C responses. You are advised to rewrite the grade-C answers to see if you can improve on the performance using the examiner's comments.

Religion and gender; church membership; New Religious Movements

Item A

Church membership in the UK (thousands)					
	1970	1995		1970	1995
Trinitarian churches			**Non-Trinitarian churches**		
Roman Catholic	2,714	1,915	Mormons	85	171
Anglican	2,994	1,785	Jehovah's Witnesses	62	131
Presbyterian	1,666	1,100	Others	138	220
Other free churches	646	648	**Other religions**		
Methodist	642	401	Muslim	130	580
Orthodox	191	289	Sikh	100	350
Baptist	269	223	Hindu	80	155
			Jewish	120	94
			Others	21	116

Source: *Social Trends*, No. 29, 1999.

(a) Identify and briefly explain **two** reasons why it could be claimed that most religions reflect a patriarchal ideology. **(8 marks)**

(b) Examine some of the reasons for the patterns of church membership shown in Item A. **(12 marks)**

(c) Assess the arguments and evidence for the view that the membership of New Religious Movements (NRMs) is drawn mainly from the poor and deprived groups in society. **(40 marks)**

Total: 60 marks

■ ■ ■

Answer to question 1: grade-A candidate

(a) The view expressed is a feminist view of religion. One reason this could be argued is that most of the world's major religions have practices that discriminate against women. For example, in many cases women are not allowed to worship at the same time or in the same place as men, as in a mosque or a Jewish synagogue, and there are many rituals that prescribe women's behaviour, such as having to wear a veil or cover her head. Other beliefs associate women with being 'unclean', particularly during menstruation or after childbirth.

Another reason is that women are seldom the leaders or holders of spiritual power. Generally, priests or holy people are male, and most gods or 'divine beings' are depicted as men. Feminists point to evidence which suggests that many ancient religions had powerful female priestesses, but that these religions were suppressed by the later, patriarchal religions, in which the position of women was down-graded.

> Two acceptable reasons are given and each is explained. It is not always necessary to write as much as this, but as long as sufficient time is left for the higher-mark questions, there is no penalty for doing so.   2 + 2 + 2 + 2 = 8/8 marks

(b) Item A compares membership of various religious groups in 1970 and 1995. It is apparent that membership of the Trinitarian churches has fallen significantly in this 25-year period, with particularly large falls for both the Roman Catholic and Anglican churches, the Anglican membership having fallen by well over a million. The Presbyterian, Methodist and Baptist churches, though with much smaller membership to start with, have still lost a significant proportion of their members. Only 'Orthodox' and 'Other free churches' have increased their membership.

> This is a good start which shows interpretation and understanding of the first part of the table. The comment about the fall in Anglican membership of 'well over a million' shows that the candidate understands that the figures are in thousands.

If we start by taking the figures at their face value, it would suggest that there is a crisis of membership in the churches mentioned. One of the reasons put forward for this is the increased secularisation of society, that is, religious beliefs, practices and institutions are losing their social significance. This is happening, it is argued, because society has become more 'rational', and people accept scientific expla-nations for a variety of phenomena rather than the reasons that once were provided by the church. A counter-argument is that people are still 'religious' but choose not to join or worship at churches, a process that Grace Davie has called 'believing, not belonging'.

> This is a strong paragraph which shows good knowledge and understanding and which offers two different explanations for the loss of membership shown in Item A. The phrase about taking the figures at face value suggests that an evaluative point about the statistics will be made later.

However, the figures relate to 'membership' of the churches, which implies a formal process of joining, probably through baptism, infant or adult, or some other manner of formal registration. It is possible that some people actually do consider themselves 'members' of the churches mentioned, and may attend services on a regular basis, but are not formally registered. In addition, as has been mentioned earlier, a decline in membership, even if real, does not necessarily tell us that there is a decline in spirituality.

🖉 The candidate demonstrates some good evaluation here, both by showing possible shortcomings in the statistics and by questioning the link between membership and religiosity. Note that the answer is already quite long, and has not yet addressed the other parts of Item A. Always keep track of time and avoid spending too long answering the lower-mark questions.

Item A also shows us that all the Non-Trinitarian churches have shown a significant increase in membership over the same period, with both the Mormons and Jehovah's Witnesses doubling their membership. One explanation for this is offered by postmodernists, who say that the lack of 'certainties' and the availability of choice in postmodern society are threatening for some people, hence the rise in membership of those religious groups who have fixed, even harsh, rules and whose doctrine claims to offer the absolute truth.

🖉 This succinct but significant paragraph again shows good interpretation of Item A and offers a sociological explanation for the pattern.

Finally, Item A shows very significant increases in the membership of 'Other religions', with the exception of the Jewish faith. Loss of members in British Jewry is attributed to the fact that 'Jewishness' is bestowed by the mother, and there is a growing tendency for Jewish men to marry Gentile women. The Muslim, Sikh and Hindu religions are, of course, particularly associated with ethnic minority groups, and there has been a significant growth in the number of immigrants practising these religions over the period shown.

🖉 Again, there is excellent interpretation of Item A, including a brief discussion of the group that does not conform to the trend in the figures.

However, the increase in the number of people from ethnic minorities does not entirely explain the increase in membership. We have to ask ourselves why people would choose membership of their religion? Part of the answer lies in the fact that, for many members of ethnic minorities, their religion provides much more than spiritual guidance. It serves as a source of identity, contributes to the transmission of their culture to the younger generation and also, in many cases, plays an important social and community role, offering secular as well as religious guidance and support. This is often particularly true for newly arrived immigrant women, who may feel particularly isolated and cut off, particularly if they do not speak English.

🖉 The candidate makes a very good evaluative point here about some of the reasons why membership of 'immigrant' religions should be so strong. At the same time there is ample evidence of good knowledge and understanding.

Overall, this is an extremely detailed and well-argued answer to part (b), albeit longer than many students would be able to produce under exam conditions. Read it through, select the main points, and see if you can come up with an A-grade answer which is somewhat shorter than this.   **12/12 marks**

question

(c) Much interest has been shown by sociologists lately in New Religious Movements, as some argue that their existence is evidence that the process of secularisation, if it is occurring at all, is taking place within the mainstream European churches and does not apply to other religious groups.

> This is an interesting and perhaps unusual start which does not go straight to the point of the question, but gives one reason why NRMs are of interest to sociologists. This shows that there is no single 'right' way of beginning an answer. However, it is unwise to wait too long before addressing the central concerns of the question, as in some cases this might be wasting valuable time.

'New Religious Movements' is an umbrella term which some sociologists prefer to 'sects and cults', as it can also apply to religious groups which are difficult to classify. NRMs exist outside of the mainstream churches, and the term covers a wide variety of groups, differing in size, beliefs, practices and orientation to the world. This makes it impossible to make statements which apply to all NRMs.

> This useful paragraph shows relevant knowledge and understanding and points out some of the problems with using the term NRMs.

The view that membership of such groups is drawn mainly from the 'poor and deprived' stems from the fact that some NRMs preach a message of hope for such marginalised people, perhaps suggesting that their difficulties in this world are a way of God testing their faith, and promising that earthly wrongs will be put right in the next world. Some American evangelical groups with a largely black membership attach great value to such beliefs, which Weber referred to as the 'theodicy of disprivilege'. In Britain, Pryce showed that Afro-Caribbeans had a high level of support for Black Pentecostalism, which Bruce argued can be used as a form of 'cultural defence' for Afro-Caribbean ethnicity.

> The answer now gets to the heart of the question, offering an explanation for the stated view, and introducing relevant sociological concepts. Good examples are given to illustrate the point being made.

As well as offering a moral justification for earthly sufferings, such groups can also provide members with much-needed solidarity and a sense of 'belonging'. To the extent that membership of and participation in such groups can deaden the pain of oppression and exclusion from the wider society, we could say that they support Marx's view of religion serving as the 'opium of the people'. Some historians have claimed that the success of the Methodist movement among the working class is one of the main reasons why there was no social revolution in Britain in the eighteenth century.

> Further reasons are given in support of the view that NRMs can offer something to marginalised groups in society. The candidate cites an interesting historical example, showing that knowledge from other subjects can sometimes be drawn on to good effect.

However, not all NRMs have a membership base among the lower classes. Walliss has suggested that sects can be 'world-affirming' or 'world-rejecting', and examples of both these types can be shown to draw members from the middle classes rather than the poor and deprived. For example, world-affirming movements such as Scientology and many of the so-called 'New Age' religions draw on a mainly middle-class membership, and profess to show members how to achieve worldly success and personal fulfilment.

☑ In this evaluative paragraph the candidate produces evidence to challenge the claim made in the question about the social characteristics of members of NRMs.

With regard to world-rejecting movements, as far back as the 1970s, many middle-class college-educated young people chose to 'drop out' and join various Utopian movements, many of them based on Eastern religions and philosophies. More recently, Eileen Barker's study of the Moonies showed that members were predominantly middle class.

☑ Further evaluation is backed up with another example of groups whose membership does not fit the profile outlined in the question.

Finally, there are movements whose membership is drawn from across the social spectrum. Many of these are linked to ethnic identity, a good example being the Nation of Islam. While its origins are rooted in 'Black Pride' and the American civil rights movement, its membership, particularly in the United States, has recently sought to draw in black professionals as well as those on the margins of society.

☑ This is an interesting evaluative point offering evidence that membership of NRMs can be socially diverse, rather than 'either/or'.

In conclusion, while some arguments and evidence support the view expressed in the question, others refute it. This is largely due to the fact that the term 'New Religious Movements' covers such a wide variety of groups, and no one explanation can fit them all.

☑ This conclusion not only summarises the material presented but offers an explanation of why it is impossible to make general statements about NRMs.

Overall, in AO1 terms the answer (c) shows very good sociological knowledge and understanding throughout, and remains clearly focused on the demands of the question. While much of the discussion is based on empirical examples, some understanding is shown of the theoretical context. In terms of AO2 requirements, the candidate clearly demonstrates the skills of identification, analysis, interpretation and evaluation, applying them to a range of sociological ideas and evidence. The answer shows a clear rationale in its structure, and the conclusion arises logically from what has gone before.   AO1: 18/20 + AO2: 18/20 = **36/40 marks**

Overall: 56/60 marks

Answer to question 1: grade-C candidate

(a) One reason is that in all the major religions, God or the supreme being of that religion is referred to as 'He', and is shown as a male figure, e.g. with a beard. Feminists say that this is patriarchal because it implies that all spiritual power is masculine in origin. Another reason is that priests and religious figures are usually men.

> Two appropriate reasons are identified, but only the first is explained. The mark is therefore 2 + 2 + 2 + 0. **6/8 marks**

(b) Item A shows that most of the Trinitarian churches lost members between 1970 and 1995. There are now less than 2 million members for both the Anglican and Roman Catholic churches. One of the main reasons for this is secularisation, that is, people are less likely to belong to a church than they used to be. Some sociologists argue that this is because people have lost their religious feelings, while others say that that they still have faith, but do not choose to belong to a church. Also, some people may be religious and may go to church, but may not be a member, so wouldn't appear in the figures. Some of the other groups, like Methodists and Baptists, haven't lost as many members, though they still show a fall. This could be because these religions tend to be based on converts, while Anglicans and Roman Catholics are usually born into the church.

> The candidate makes a reasonably good start which identifies some information about changes in church membership from Item A and offers a possible reason for them. It would help to give an example of a sociologist for each of the two positions with regard to the secularisation debate. There is a hint of evaluation in the distinction between church attendance and church membership. While it is true that Methodists and Baptists have not lost as many members as Anglicans and Roman Catholics, their membership was much smaller to begin with, so what is more important is the proportional decline. Always think carefully about what statistics are showing. The reasoning behind the possible explanation based on conversion versus ascription is not made clear.

On the other hand, Mormons and Jehovah's Witnesses have both increased their members. One reason for this is that both these groups work hard to recruit members, and membership of sects is growing, especially in the United States. Some people join these groups because they feel that the mainstream religions have failed them.

> Again, some information is extracted from Item A and an attempt is made to explain it. The candidate gives no evidence for the alleged increase in membership of sects, and the figures in the table relate to the UK, so reference to the United States does not assist the argument, unless its relevance to UK figures is shown. A potentially relevant point is made about why some people might join such groups, but it is not developed.

The other thing shown in Item A is an increase in membership of other religions, especially Muslim, Sikh and Hindu. This is because these religions are usually found among members of ethnic minority groups, and there has been a big increase in the number of immigrants belonging to these religions over the last 30 years.

> Relevant information is taken from Item A, although no note is made of the fact that membership of the Jewish religion has fallen. The point about the link between the religions mentioned and ethnic minority groups should have been explored further, for example by discussing the role of religion in these communities.

Overall, the information in Item A shows that most of the religions followed by white Britons have lost members, while those followed by ethnic minorities have increased. The figures reflect our multicultural society, and show differences between the host and immigrant groups in terms of religiosity. If ethnic minorities take on the characteristics of the host society, and become more secular, membership of their religions might start to fall in the future.

> This is a fairly weak and simplistic conclusion, which adds little to what has gone before. The point about 'white Britons' is ill-advised, as such people make up a considerable proportion of the membership of Mormons and Jehovah's Witnesses. The assumption is made that church membership figures tell us something about 'religiosity', though a reference in an earlier paragraph shows us that the student is aware of possible problems in interpreting the statistics. An interesting point is made regarding possible future changes.

> Overall, some relevant information is taken from the table, and the candidate attempts to explain some of the findings. The concepts of 'secularisation' and 'religiosity' are introduced but are not explored in any depth. There is some very limited evaluation. **5/12 marks**

(c) New Religious Movements is the name given by some sociologists to a variety of sects and cults that have grown up outside of the 'mainstream' churches. Membership of NRMs has grown in recent years, which some say proves that secularisation is not taking place, as although people are leaving the churches, a lot of them are joining NRMs.

> This is a promising start, which shows knowledge of what is meant by New Religious Movements and of the fact that their membership has increased. However, the introduction of the concept of secularisation is ominous — it is to be hoped that the answer will not drift away from the question into a discussion of the role of NRMs in the debate about secularisation. Remember that good answers stay firmly focused on the set question.

NRMs take a variety of forms. Walliss says that they can be world-affirming, world-rejecting or world-accommodating. Many of them have charismatic leaders, like the Reverend Sun Myung Moon of the Moonies. Some NRMs are very short-lived, while others, like the Moonies, last for much longer. Some have thousands of members, while others are very small, with only a handful of people.

> While this paragraph offers accurate information about NRMs, there is still no attempt to address the central point of the question, namely the social characteristics of the people who join them.

Some sociologists argue that NRMs appear in times of acute social change and upheaval, when many people become anxious and feel unable to cope. NRMs, it is suggested, recruit members by promising certainty and security. However, research has shown that not all NRMs appear at such times, and not all people join them to get emotional security.

> This begins to touch on the issue of membership, but there is still no clear focus. An evaluative point is made regarding the emergence of NRMs.

Weber suggested that NRMs would appeal most to the poor and underprivileged members of society, who would gain a sense of belonging and would respond to claims that suffering in this world would be put right in the next one, thus offering members hope for the future. This is probably true for some NRMs, e.g. those joined by poor American blacks, who were marginalised by the American system, and the Native American Ghost Dancers, who believed that the magic made them immune to white men's bullets, but other NRMs attract a more middle-class clientele, such as those joined by hippies in the 1970s and Scientologists more recently.

> At last the answer gets to the central issue, giving reasons why the poor and underprivileged might join NRMs, and making the evaluative point that not all members of NRMs fall into this category.

Eileen Barker studied the Moonies, a sect that had been accused of brain-washing its members and not allowing them to leave. Barker used triangulation in her research, employing participant observation and questionnaires. She found that members were not brain-washed, and could leave if they wanted. Many of the Moonies she spoke to were from middle-class supportive families.

> There is much potentially relevant information in this paragraph but it is not used to best advantage. The point about Barker's methodology is not used to develop any argument, and thus adds nothing, while the important point about the middle-class origins of members is simply stated and not used as evidence to counteract the view put forward in the question.

Postmodernists suggest that religion is now 'pick'n'mix', with people selecting the ideas and practices that suit their needs, which means that the door is open for even more NRMs, as new ones spring up to meet a growing variety of needs. Some will be client-based and others audience-based. Bruce says that membership of these New Age movements is mainly middle class, as working-class people don't have the time or the money to join in.

🖉 Again, this paragraph contains promising material, but it is not used to address the question. The point about Bruce's views on 'New Age' group membership is obviously an important one, but the candidate loses marks by not stating explicitly that this undermines the view expressed in the question.

Membership of NRMs is drawn from a wide variety of backgrounds, therefore it is not possible to say that members come mainly from the poor and deprived groups in society.

🖉 This brief conclusion is only thinly supported by the preceding discussion, but it does at least offer a clear answer to the question about NRM membership.

This answer to part (c) displays some relevant AO1 knowledge and understanding of NRMs, and some limited understanding of the demands of the question. There is quite a lot of potentially relevant information here, much of which is not developed or used to focus on the question. AO2 skills are shown but in a somewhat limited fashion. There is a lack of clear structure to the answer, in that the points do not always follow logically from each other. The focus tends to be on the general topic area rather than on the set question. There is limited analysis of the arguments and evidence presented. Some evaluative points are made, but these are not developed.　　　　　　AO1: 11/20 + AO2: 9/20 = **20/40 marks**

Overall: 31/60 marks

Religion and moral guidance; religion and social change; secularisation

Item A

For Steve Bruce, the prospects for religion in the modern world are not good at all. As he sees it, Christianity has been in a state of decline in the UK for at least the last 150 years and definitely over the course of the last century. During the twentieth century, church attendances dropped from almost 30% of the population to 10%. In the same period, the number of children attending Sunday schools — once the only form of education for many children — fell from 55% of the population to just 4%. Not only are those who attend religious services predominantly in older age groups but, perhaps more importantly, there is little empirical evidence for any significant religiosity amongst the young who could one day replace them.

Source: adapted from J. Walliss, 'The Secularisation Debate', *Sociology Review*, September 2002.

(a) Identify and briefly explain two criticisms of the view that religion is no longer a source of moral guidance in society. (8 marks)

(b) Examine some of the ways in which religious beliefs can promote social change. (12 marks)

(c) Using information from Item A and elsewhere, assess the arguments and evidence for the view that there is much more religiosity in society than the secularisation theorists acknowledge. (40 marks)

Total: 60 marks

■ ■ ■

Answer to question 2: grade-A candidate

(a) One criticism of this view is that it is far too general. While it may be true that some people do not immediately, if at all, turn to their religion or religious leaders for guidance on moral issues, it is equally true that many people do see their faith as not necessarily 'a' source but 'the' source of moral guidance. Examples would include those Roman Catholics who follow the teachings of their church on issues of birth control, abortion and divorce, and devout Muslims, Hindus and Jews who try to live their daily lives according to the teachings of their religious leaders. In addition, it would appear that many people who are not normally 'religious' still turn to their church in times of trouble, as happened in the USA after the terrorist attacks of 11 September 2001.

A further criticism arises out of the phrase 'no longer'. Hill, for example, argues that the medieval period should not be seen as an 'age of faith', and sociologists such as Stark point to evidence showing widespread apathy to religion among the population in earlier centuries. Many of the clergy were ignorant of doctrinal teachings, and even when people did go to church they went unwillingly, and behaved in ways that we would consider quite inappropriate. The extent to which the mass of people ever did look to religion as a source of moral guidance is therefore debatable.

> This answer is very detailed, and perhaps longer than it need be to get the marks. However, two appropriate criticisms are identified, and each is explained and briefly discussed. The example about turning to religion for comfort in times of trouble or crisis is not really relevant to the issue of 'moral guidance', but there is already sufficient other material to gain full marks.   2 + 2 + 2 + 2 = **8/8 marks**

(b) The most influential writer on the issue of the relationship between religion and social change is Weber. In his book 'The Protestant Ethic and the Spirit of Capitalism', Weber tried to show how the religious ideas of seventeenth-century Calvinists led to attitudes and behaviour that were favourable to the development of capitalist modes of production. In particular, Weber emphasised the importance of the Calvinist view of work as a 'calling', something that should be undertaken willingly and vigorously as a way of honouring God, and their view that life should be lived in as simple a fashion as possible, with no conspicuous consumption. The combination of these two values led to a thrifty, hard-working group of people who amassed sufficient capital to develop new ideas and inventions, thus paving the way for the development of capitalist modes of production.

> This is a good introductory paragraph which gets straight to the point of the question. Weber's ideas are briefly summarised, and two particular religious values are identified and shown to link to the development of capitalism and thus social change.

Weber thus attempted to show that religious ideas could facilitate social, political and economic change, although he did not state that Protestantism of itself 'caused' capitalism.

> Three different aspects of social change linked to Calvinist ideas are identified, and the important point is made that Weber was not claiming that there was a causal link between religious ideas and social change.

Another example of links between religious ideas and social change is that of the Latin-American 'liberation theologists', worker-priests who saw it as their Christian duty to oppose injustice and wrong-doing and try, by revolutionary means if neces-sary, to bring about a better and fairer society. In so doing, they rejected the Christian value of meekness and 'turning the other cheek'.

> Another relevant example is given of a link between a religious group and an attempt to bring about social change.

question

Similarly, other religious groups, such as some of the Christian Black Power movements, actively used their religious beliefs and networks to work for social change and improvements for black Americans, while there are examples of militant groups such as Al Qaida, Hiz Bollah and Hamas which link their religious views with nationalist causes, and see their struggle as a 'holy war'.

🖉 These further examples show a good breadth of knowledge on this topic.

However, there are other views on this question. Marx, for example, believed that religion was essentially a conservative force in society, as it was used in an ideological sense to justify the superior position of the ruling class. Another example of religion as a conservative force is the Hindu caste system, in which people were taught to accept the position into which they were born and follow all the caste rules, in the belief that in their next life they would be born into a higher social position.

🖉 Evaluation is demonstrated by introducing counter-arguments, with an example to show religion acting as a conservative force.

Where a particular religion is adopted as the state religion, it also usually acts to maintain the status quo in society. Fundamentalism provides an interesting example, as fundamentalist ideas can be a force for social change, as in the Iranian revolution of the Ayatollah Khomenei, but once in power, fundamentalist regimes can be ultra-conservative and inhibit any other social change by giving supreme authority to religious leaders such as the Taliban.

🖉 The example of fundamentalism is used in both an analytical and an evaluative way to further the debate about religion and social change.

Finally, some have questioned the ability of religious ideas to bring about social change, arguing that an overemphasis on religion can lead to the neglect of other important factors, such as non-religious political movements or economic conditions in bringing about change in society.

🖉 This is a further evaluative point, acknowledging the possible importance of other factors.

However, religious ideas can be shown to promote social change, but can also be shown in other circumstances to act as a conservative force in society.

🖉 Although brief, this conclusion neatly sums up the arguments and evidence presented in the answer.

Overall, the candidate demonstrates the A-level skills successfully in this answer. Analysis and evaluation are made explicit, and knowledge and understanding are both very sound. The answer stays focused on the issue of religious beliefs and social change, and a range of appropriate examples are used to support the arguments made. **12/12 marks**

(c) Item A gives some of the views and evidence put forward by those sociologists who believe that modern western societies are undergoing a process of 'secularisation'. The most commonly accepted definition of secularisation is that of Wilson, who said that secularisation was a process in which 'religious beliefs, institutions and practices lose their social significance'.

⟮e⟯ This is a good introductory paragraph which identifies the views in Item A and offers the standard definition of secularisation, the crucial concept in this question.

Briefly, we should look at the reasons why some sociologists believe that secularisation is taking place, and then at the evidence they present to prove their case. One of the main theoretical reasons stems from the work of Weber, who held that belief in religion would decline as society became more 'rational', that is, as scientific ideas and evidence replaced beliefs based on magic and superstition. This process has been termed 'disenchantment' or 'demystification'. It is true that scientists are gradually uncovering some of the most essential 'mysteries', with their explanations of natural phenomena such as droughts and earthquakes and their ability to understand and in some cases cure disease, as well as being able to 'create' life outside the womb in a test tube.

⟮e⟯ The candidate is presenting the case for secularisation first, with the idea, presumably, of addressing the counter-argument based on the degree of religiosity later. This is quite acceptable as a strategy, provided that you remember not to spend too long on this first part before showing the examiner that you are addressing the central issue(s) of the question. Here, one aspect of secularisation is discussed, using an appropriate sociological concept together with a supporting example.

Another reason offered for the growth of secularisation is the growing separation of Church and state, referring to the declining power of religious institutions. This process is known as 'disengagement', and is shown by the greatly weakened ability of the Church in governing the country. Some argue that despite some Bishops sitting in the House of Lords, the role of the Church of England in matters of state is largely relegated to providing pageant and ritual, for example at coronations and royal funerals.

⟮e⟯ Another aspect and concept are introduced, with a relevant example.

Finally, the idea is put forward that the rise of consumerism and a postmodern society has led to people having a wide range of choices with regard to their identity, lifestyle and belief system, choices that people in earlier times did not have. In such a society, it is argued that religion and religious beliefs and practices are just one option available to people, and some people in society will reject them.

⟮e⟯ An attempt is made to link secularisation to postmodernity and consumerism, though the argument is perhaps not as clear as it might be.

question

With regard to the evidence that the believers in secularisation put forward, some of this is given in Item A. Falling church and Sunday school attendances and the age-profile of church attenders are all produced as evidence. In addition, the pro-secularisation theorists point to the decline in people training for the priesthood, the fall in marriages taking place in church, the decline in infant baptisms and the flouting of what many see as the basic principles of Christian behaviour, e.g. kindness, tolerance, forgiveness and 'moral' conduct. Overall, then, the secularisation theorists such as Bruce and Wilson believe that religion and religiosity are both in decline.

> Here the candidate summarises the kinds of evidence put forward by the secularisation theorists, with a concluding sentence to remind us of what the preceding paragraphs have been attempting to show.

However, this position has been attacked on several fronts. One of the anomalies in the debate is that surveys repeatedly show that, while people may no longer go to church in significant numbers, a majority of people still profess a belief in God, a god or some spiritual force. As Davie has said, they believe, even though they no longer belong. Another criticism is that the evidence of falling religious attendance and membership is based largely on the main Christian Trinitarian churches, ignoring the different pattern shown by non-Trinitarian churches such as the Mormons and Jehovah's Witnesses and those faiths followed by members of Britain's ethnic minority communities, which are showing increases in membership and which play a significant role in the daily lives of their members.

> Some relevant counter-evidence is produced to criticise the secularisation theorists.

So, does this anti-secularisation evidence show that there is still 'religiosity' in society? One of the fundamental problems here is which definition of 'religion' is adopted. Inclusivist definitions of religion are so all-embracing that it can be argued that everyone has a degree of 'religiosity', even if they profess no faith at all and never go near a place of worship. This view is obviously unhelpful to the present debate, and the majority of sociologists accept some kind of exclusivist definition of religion, which draws the boundaries more tightly.

> The answer now addresses the central concept of religiosity, and shows evaluation by pointing out the problems arising from definitions of religion.

What do we mean, then, by 'religiosity' and how do we measure it? If religiosity means having some kind of religious or spiritual belief, then the evidence would tend to point to the existence of religiosity in the majority of the population. If religiosity means having to demonstrate religious belief by some kind of ritual or practice, then a smaller number of people would be deemed to be religious. However, this number would still cover a sizeable proportion of the population, as it would have to include non-Trinitarian, non-Christian faiths and practices.

✐ This is a good evaluative point showing that the definition of religiosity will determine its extent in society.

Wilson has argued that we have seen the rise of what he calls 'civil religions', that is, religious beliefs linked to ideas of nationality. Religious-type symbolism and rituals are used on secular occasions, such as the swearing-in of a president or at football matches, particularly when national teams are playing. In this view, 'religiosity' is present, but not linked to specifically religious beliefs.

✐ Another view of 'religiosity' is presented, giving further evidence of the problems of definition.

Writers such as Iannacconne and Stark have criticised the concept and evidence of secularisation as being highly Eurocentric. They point, as others have done, to the fact that the evidence is based largely on the Christian churches of medieval Europe, but go on to say that a more accurate picture is given by looking at the United States. Religion in the United States is powerful and flourishing and is not, they argue, a secularised, Disneyfied form of religion, but is deeply meaningful to those involved. They point in particular to the spectacular success of the Mormon church in recruiting and maintaining members, not just in America but throughout the world. In this view, 'real' religiosity is present among huge numbers of people. Other evidence from the USA would be the power of the so-called New Christian Right, whose members ally deeply held religious beliefs to strong political views and action and represent a powerful force in American politics.

✐ The views of Iannacconne and Stark are used to criticise some of the basic assumptions and evidence in the pro-secularisation debate.

Other writers argue that there is a fundamental need for some kind of religiosity in humans, and if it is not met by conventional means it will be fulfilled elsewhere. Hence the idea of the 'Gods of the Gaps' — the view that, for example, certain 'celebrities' can become substitutes for religious icons.

✐ The candidate produces another example to show how apparently non-religious factors can be linked to religiosity.

The rise in so-called 'New Age' movements has also been put forward as evidence of religiosity in society, even though not directly linked to formal religious organisations. However, Bruce points out that these are largely followed by middle-class professionals seeking 'self-improvement' or 'self-realisation', and are literally 'self-centred', so cannot properly be used as evidence of religiosity as the term is usually interpreted. Rather, he argues, they show how individualistic society has become, whereas some of the early religious movements such as the Quakers and Methodists reflected a desire to contribute to, and improve, society as a whole.

✐ Another example of something that is claimed to show increased religiosity is followed by an appropriate critique.

In conclusion, then, as with many sociological debates, much depends on the definition applied to particular concepts (in this case, 'secularisation' and 'religiosity') and also on how the evidence is interpreted. Secularisation theorists such as Wilson and Bruce will continue to argue that most of the evidence put forward to show that there are still high levels of religiosity does not, in fact, show this at all. Those such as Martin and possibly Davie who argue against the view that society is less 'religious' than formerly will continue to defend their arguments, generally giving a different interpretation to the evidence. No doubt all those involved would agree that religious practices and possibly even religious beliefs have changed, but would continue to disagree over what this means for individuals and society.

> This thoughtful conclusion summarises the problems of many sociological debates, but stays focused on the question.

> Overall, the candidate demonstrates very sound sociological knowledge and understanding, and interprets the question well. The answer covers both theoretical and empirical aspects, and stays focused. ˙A range of appropriate material is introduced, and there is evidence of both analysis and evaluation. This answer shows that it is possible to gain full marks for a question.
> AO1: 20/20 + AO2: 20/20 = **40/40 marks**

> **Overall: 60/60 marks**

■ ■ ■

Answer to question 2: grade-C candidate

(a) One criticism is that many people do get moral guidance from their religion. Roman Catholics, for example, believe that divorce and abortion are wrong as they are against the teachings of the church.
Another criticism is that some people argue that people have always disobeyed the teachings of the church, so you can't say 'no longer'.

> The first point is identified and explained by use of an example, so the candidate gains 2 marks for each of these. However, a second potentially relevant criticism is identified, but no further explanation is given, so it is not possible to award marks for this. This answer is therefore worth 2 + 2 + 2 + 0. **6/8 marks**

(b) This is really a debate between Weber and Marx. Weber used the ideas of the Protestant ethic and the spirit of capitalism to show that religion could bring about social change, while Marx believed that religion was a conservative force in society.

> This is a promising start that locates the question in a theoretical context.

Weber looked at how the ideas of Calvinists helped to bring about industrial capitalism. Calvinists were members of a strict Christian sect that believed that people should live a frugal life and should not spend money on unnecessary luxuries. Because they also believed in hard work, they tended to make a lot of money, and many of them were business entrepreneurs. As they didn't spend their money on goods, they tended to plough it back into their businesses. This meant that when the industrial revolution required a huge investment of capital, there was a group of people in society with a good work ethic and, just as important, the means at their disposal to make these investments.

e Although awkwardly expressed in places, this is a basically sound account of the Protestant ethic and its link to capitalism.

So although the Protestant ethic didn't cause capitalism, Weber said that it provided the necessary moral and economic climate for capitalism to develop. As the industrial revolution and capitalism brought about huge social changes, Weber had made the link between religious ideas and social change.

e The candidate sums up the relationship between a particular set of religious ideas and social change, linking this clearly to the question.

Another way that religion can bring about social change is liberation theology. This took place in Latin America, where some priests and nuns taught the people that they should not accept their lot as 'God's will' but should actively work to change things for the better. Many priests and nuns were persecuted for these teachings, but it shows how religion does not always act as a conservative force to maintain the status quo. Some Christian charities also work to try to improve people's lives in developing countries, either through providing things such as education and medicine, or by campaigning against practices that harm people, such as the use of land mines.

e Two further examples illustrate the link between religious beliefs and social change, although this link is left somewhat implicit in the second example.

One problem with this is that social change is very complex, and it is not usually possible to identify one single thing that brings it about. This is why we have to be careful not to say that just one thing 'causes' social change, though it might be trying to achieve it. For example, although the Christian charity workers might be trying to promote change by providing schools, the government of the country might get a loan to invest more in education, so the change would have come from more than one source, not just charity.

e This important evaluative paragraph attempts to show that 'promoting' and 'causing' social change are not the same thing.

So, while some religious ideas do act to keep the society static, at other times religious ideas can be used to bring about, or try to bring about, social change.

e The candidate concludes with a reminder that religious ideas can act as both a conservative force and as a force for social change.

The answer to part (b) demonstrates reasonably sound knowledge and under-standing of the issues raised by the question, with some relevant theoretical as well as empirical material. There is some explicit evaluation, while elsewhere evaluation is more by juxtaposition. **7/12 marks**

(c) As Item A shows, some sociologists, such as Steve Bruce, argue that secularisa-tion is taking place in modern Britain. Bruce believes that Christianity has been in a state of decline in the UK for at least the last 150 years. One of the main reasons for believing this is the fact that church membership and church atten-dance have both shown a dramatic fall, with only 10% of the population now regularly attending church.

> Reference is made to Item A, but too much of this opening paragraph is simply copied from it, and very little is added. Remember that information from the source material should be interpreted, not simply copied or paraphrased.

As Item A says, more evidence regarding secularisation comes from a fall in the number of children attending Sunday school, as well as falls in children getting baptised, marriages taking place in church and people training for the priesthood. Sundays have stopped being days set aside for religious purposes, and we now live in a 24/7 society, where many shops are open all week and people can take part in a wide variety of leisure pursuits on Sunday. Many people have to work on Sundays.

> This paragraph gives further evidence of the UK becoming a more secular society, but presents it in rather a list-like way.

Sociologists have put forward a number of reasons for the increase in seculari-sation. Marx believed that religion would inevitably die as socialism overthrew capitalism. Weber argued that, with industrialisation and the rise of modernity, society would become more rational, and belief in non-scientific explanations, including religious ones, would decline (disenchantment). Others have suggested that as the state grew more powerful, the power and the influence of the church would inevitably decline, and the state would take over many of the roles previ-ously played by the church (disengagement). Formal education for everyone, replacing Sunday school, as shown in Item A, is an example of this. Postmodernists argue that in postmodern society there is no place for 'meta-narratives', of which religion is an example, and say that in societies characterised by choice, people will choose to have no religion, or will select from a variety of religious beliefs to find those that suit their own individual lifestyle.

> The sociological concepts of disenchantment and disengagement are introduced to give further reasons for the increase in secularisation, but there is a danger that this answer is going down the road of offering a general discussion on 'secularisa-tion', rather than focusing on the question set. Always ensure that you make clear how the points made in your answer are relevant to the question.

However, not everyone accepts that secularisation is taking place. Evidence shows that although the major Christian churches are in decline in the UK, other religions and other groups are increasing their members. This suggests that people might be just turning away from the major churches, rather than from religion itself.

☑ The candidate brings in a hint of evaluation by criticising the view that secularisation is occurring. It would have been a good idea to provide examples of religions and groups increasing their members, rather than just stating that this is the case. The answer has yet to introduce and discuss the concept of 'religiosity' in the question.

Bellah and Luckmann both argue that religion has become a more 'private' affair, on an individual level of meaning (individuation), so looking at church attendances doesn't necessarily show how 'religious' society is. Also important is the notion of 'civil religion', where secular events and activities take on an almost religious meaning. This is especially true where the event is one that appears to bring 'the people' together, and/or where the event can be used to reinforce national pride and solidarity. Examples might be the funeral of Princess Diana, supporting England in the World Cup, celebrating the Queen's Jubilee or, in the USA, celebrating Independence Day. The terrorist attacks of 11 September 2001 also brought American citizens together in almost religious fervour.

☑ There is potentially some very useful material here, but it is not explicitly linked to the notion of 'religiosity'. Think of an introductory sentence to this paragraph which would provide an appropriate focus for the material presented. An evaluative point is made regarding the problem of measuring secularisation by looking at church attendances.

Further evidence against secularisation exists in the fact that surveys repeatedly show that, even if they don't take part in formal worship, most people still have a faith or belief in God, or at least some spiritual or supernatural being. Davie has called this 'believing, not belonging', which shows that religiosity is still present even though some of the evidence presented by the secularisation theorists seems to indicate otherwise.

☑ At last there is a mention of the all-important concept of 'religiosity', and some evidence in support of it.

In conclusion, it is difficult to judge the nature and extent of secularisation. There is no agreed definition, and the evidence can be interpreted in different ways. Church attendance statistics are flawed, and in any case may not be an appropriate way of measuring the amount of religiosity in society. People may be choosing to express their religious feelings in different ways.

☑ In terms of the wording of the question, it would have been better had the focus of the conclusion been on 'religiosity' rather than 'secularisation'. Nevertheless, there is an attempt to answer the question.

Overall, in AO1 terms, this answer to part (c) shows reasonably good sociological knowledge and understanding, although this is sometimes at the level of the general topic area rather than the specific issues raised by the question. A range of material is presented, both empirical and theoretical (more the former than the latter), and some appropriate concepts are introduced. Regarding AO2 skills, the identification of perspectives and arguments is accurate, though these are not always interpreted to show their relevance to the set question. There is relatively little analysis, but some evaluative points are made, though not developed.

AO1: 11/20 + AO2: 8/20 = **19/40 marks**

Overall: 32/60 marks

Sects; fundamentalism; the functions of religion

Item A

The growing support for the ideas of fundamentalism has also presented new issues for the secularisation thesis. Davie argues that the term is often incorrectly used when applied in a negative way about Christian sects or Islam, implying that they are the bizarre religions of fanatics. In fact, sociologists ought to use the term fundamentalism as a descriptive word that is concerned with certain kinds of religious movement in the contemporary, postmodern world. It describes a desire to promote a return to the basic truths of a well-established religion. The emergence of fundamentalism on a large scale and across several continents in recent years has bewildered many commentators. It has questioned common sociological assumptions that the contemporary world is becoming more secular.

Source: adapted from P. Selfe and M. Starbuck, *Access to Sociology: Religion*, Hodder and Stoughton, 1998.

(a) **Identify and explain *two* reasons why some sects are short-lived.** (8 marks)

(b) **With reference to material from Item A and elsewhere, examine some of the reasons for the apparent increase in religious fundamentalism.** (12 marks)

(c) **Assess the arguments and evidence for the view that the functions once performed by religion have been taken over by other social agencies.** (40 marks)

Total: 60 marks

■ ■ ■

Answer to question 3: grade-A candidate

(a) One reason why some sects are short-lived is that they are relatively small and are founded on the leadership of a single charismatic leader. During the active life of the sect leader, membership may grow and the sect may flourish. However, as most charismatic leaders claim to have certain special unique powers or knowledge of 'the truth', it is not usually possible to find a successor. Thus, when the charismatic leader dies or becomes too ill or frail to lead the sect, membership tends to dwindle and the sect dies out.

> 🖉 A relevant reason is identified and explained. While this answer would gain the marks (2 + 2), it would have been a good idea to include an example. Can you think of an appropriate one?

A second reason is that sect membership is mainly by conversion rather than ascription (being born into the sect). Eileen Barker's research shows that for some sects both the recruitment and retention of new members is difficult, and the sect begins to have an ageing profile. One reason for the difficulties of recruitment is that many sects require unquestioning obedience to the leader, and, in the case of some world-rejecting sects, a harsh lifestyle with no luxuries and little if any contact with the outside world, which many people find hard to endure for long periods.

📝 A second appropriate reason is identified and explained, so the candidate again obtains 2 + 2 marks, giving full marks for part (a).   **8/8 marks**

(b) As Item A indicates, fundamentalism refers to religious beliefs and practices which hold to what is regarded as the original, basic and 'fundamental' truths of a religion. The term was originally applied to those Christian groups which hold that the Bible is literally true, and that its teachings should be followed to the letter. However, 'fundamentalism' is now applied to religious groups other than Christians, particularly in the phrase 'Islamic fundamentalists'.

📝 This is a good start which selects some relevant information from Item A and goes on to display good knowledge and understanding of the term 'fundamentalism'.

Again, as Item A shows, in recent years fundamentalist movements have appeared on a large scale and in different continents, which has been used by some sociologists as further evidence to cast doubt on the secularisation thesis. If this is the case, then fundamentalism represents an important phenomenon in the sociology of religion. Some of the possible reasons for the apparent growth in fundamentalism are discussed below.

📝 Two further relevant points are selected from the source material and are then used to indicate why fundamentalism might be significant. It is always better to use the source material to develop an argument or as a starting-point to display further knowledge on the topic than simply to copy out phrases and 'let them speak for themselves'.

One possible reason for the rise of fundamentalism was put forward in an article by Andrew Holden on 'Millenarianism and postmodernity'. Using Jehovah's Witnesses as an example of both a millenarian and a fundamentalist movement, Holden argues that the success of this and other movements in a postmodern world is based at least partly on their offer of 'certainty'. One of the characteristics of postmodern society is the rejection of any single 'truth', and the availability of open-ended choices to individuals in constructing their own identity. While for some this represents freedom, for others it leads to great uncertainty and insecurity. It can therefore be comforting to believe in something where there is no room for uncertainty, to join a movement in which you are told what to believe and how to act, especially as this is linked to a belief that by doing so you will be 'saved' and will have eternal life. There are now over 6 million Witnesses, and the movement continues to grow. This argument could also be used to explain the growth of parts of the New Christian Right in America, with its firm messages about codes of moral behaviour. People are left in no doubt about what is right and wrong, and therefore know exactly how they should behave.

🖉 A good discussion is developed, showing analysis as well as knowledge and understanding. The candidate locates fundamentalism in a postmodern context and provides an example of a fundamentalist group.

Another type of fundamentalism is that found in other religions, notably Islam and Judaism. In these cases, the religious beliefs are also strongly linked to issues of identity, particularly national identity, where this is seen to be under threat from external forces.

🖉 The discussion now turns to further examples of fundamentalism, showing breadth of knowledge and understanding.

Arab and Palestinian attacks on Israel since the Six Day War have reinforced the sense of 'Jewishness' under attack, particularly as the disputed territories cover lands promised to Jews by the Bible. Jewish fundamentalist groups have gained considerable influence in Israel. Of course, the Palestinians see themselves as fighting a 'Holy War' to get the Jews out of their territory, so fundamentalist beliefs are used to support the views of both sides in the dispute.

🖉 The candidate brings in current affairs to further the discussion, while maintaining the link to a discussion of fundamentalism. It is very important to keep a tight focus on the question.

Finally, the Muslim world has seen the emergence of fundamentalist groups which attempt to make societies return to the principles of Islam after being 'corrupted' by colonial powers and the influence of the West. Those Muslims who live outside Muslim countries are also urged to live by Muslim principles and to be 'Muslim' before anything else. This emphasis on Muslim identity has caused some problems in Western societies, and has drawn attention to the possible conflicts faced by those who try to live by both the laws of Islam and the laws of their host country.

🖉 Further examples of good, relevant knowledge and understanding are firmly focused on the issue of fundamentalism. The final sentence also gives evidence of evaluation.

Therefore, some of the reasons for the increase in religious fundamentalism are the search for 'certainty' and issues of identity.

🖉 In a brief but adequate conclusion the candidate restates the factors identified in the discussion.

This is a somewhat atypical answer in terms of the particular knowledge displayed, but nevertheless one which makes good use of the source material, stays focused on the question, and shows excellent relevant knowledge and understanding, with some evidence of analysis and evaluation. **12/12 marks**

(c) The notion that religion performs certain functions for society is found in both the functionalist and Marxist views. However, while the functionalists believe that the functions performed by religion are positive and beneficial to the whole society, Marxists believe that the main function of religion is as part of the ideological state apparatus, helping to justify the privilege and power of capitalists by presenting them as 'God-given'. Marx himself also believed that religion performed the function of providing comfort for the working classes, and deadened the pain of their exploitation — religion as 'the opium of the people'.

> A general introduction briefly discusses two sociological perspectives which see religion as performing particular functions. While not yet focused on the actual question, such an introduction, if kept brief, is often useful in that it shows the examiner that you can locate the question in a particular sociological context. Make sure, however, that the answer quickly gets 'on track' with regard to the main thrust of the question.

The view expressed in the question forms part of the debate on whether or not secularisation is taking place. Although the question talks about the functions of 'religion', it is probably more accurate to talk about the functions of 'churches' or religious bodies.

> After the generalised introduction, the answer begins to address the main point of the question, and raises an interesting evaluative point arising from the wording of the question.

The early functionalists in particular, such as Durkheim and Malinowski, believed that religion, in common with other social 'organs', performed a variety of functions beneficial both to individuals and to society as a whole. Durkheim believed that religion was part of the 'sacred', i.e. things set apart and revered. It performed the vital function of offering moral guidance to members of society, teaching them right from wrong, and therefore helping to ensure that people would act according to the norms and values of their society, thus reducing conflict. This function has been described as being the 'moral glue' holding society together. Malinowski, using the example of the Trobriand Islanders, also showed how religion and religious rituals helped people to cope with stress, anxiety and danger.

> This paragraph expands on functionalist views of the role of religion, showing good knowledge and understanding.

However, historically organised religion, as expressed by the church, has performed other functions. The Christian church in medieval Europe had immense power, both spiritual and economic. It trained scholars, looked after the poor, advised monarchs and could even raise armies to fight in 'holy wars'. Even when the power of the Roman Catholic church began to diminish, particularly in England after the break with Rome, the various functions of the church were still in evidence, and its leaders and priests played important roles in society. Before the introduction in the nineteenth century of state schooling for all, Sunday schools provided a basic education for many children, and church leaders in the community would usually be involved in the administration of the Poor Law, showing that the education and welfare function of the church in Britain continued even after industrialisation.

☑ A historical note is introduced here, with examples showing other types of function performed by the Christian church, rather than 'religion' in general. This is, of course, still a legitimate way of addressing the question.

However, it is argued that as part of the general process of secularisation, disengagement is now taking place. According to Berger, disengagement is 'the process by which sectors of society and culture are removed from the domination of religious institutions and symbols'. This is the view indicated in the title of this question, where 'the functions once performed by religion have been taken over by other social agencies'.

☑ The answer now gets to the heart of the question by introducing the important concept of 'disengagement' and locating it within the secularisation debate. There is also a useful quote from Berger. While such direct quotations are not, of course, essential, if you can remember one which is relevant to your discussion, then introduce it. Even if you get a couple of words wrong, it won't matter — unless it alters the meaning of the quotation.

The argument is that as society becomes more 'rational', more bureaucratic, more scientific and more meritocratic, the state and its agencies begin to take over some of both the power and the functions of the church. But to what extent is this argument supported by evidence?

☑ The answer recognises that both 'arguments' and 'evidence' have been asked for. In such cases, it is essential to address both, though not necessarily in equal depth, to get into the top band.

It is clear that the British state has taken control of many former functions of the church. All pupils have a right to a free state education between the ages of 5 and 16, welfare benefits are administered and paid for by the state, there is a state system of health care, and the power of the church in political and economic matters is insignificant compared to what it once was.

☑ A brief but focused paragraph offers evidence for the taking over of certain functions by the state.

However, it would be wrong, and not supported by the evidence, to claim that the church has lost all of its functions. A growing number of parents of different religious beliefs choose to send their children to 'faith schools' — and indeed the government recognises the value of these and is encouraging more of them to be opened. While the church has relatively little involvement in health care in this country (though there are some church-run hospices for the dying), all the major churches and denominations are involved in education and health care in developing countries. At the level of the local community, church leaders and church workers offer help and support, both spiritual and practical, to those in need. While the power of the church in the House of Lords has declined, politicians still take note of the pronouncements of church leaders from all faiths, and these are often involved in talks designed to implement community-based policies, particularly in areas where there has been conflict, such as inner cities or the northern towns that saw inter-ethnic disturbances in the summer of 2001.

This is an evaluative paragraph showing good knowledge and understanding of the role still played by the church in many aspects of society.

It must also be recognised that Britain is a multicultural society, and for many members of ethnic minority groups the church, mosque or temple is an essential part of their community and their life, performing many of the same educational and welfare functions as the early Christian churches.

The view of Britain as a multicultural and multifaith society, and the implications of this, are often neglected in answers on religion. Make sure that you recognise this important feature of Britain in your answer.

Finally, we should perhaps look at the notion of 'civil religion' introduced by sociologists such as Bellah and Herberg. This argues that certain types of national symbolism and ritual have become like religion in that they perform the same integrating function that religion used to. Shils' article on the Queen's Coronation in 1952 was an example of this, and more recent examples might include the funeral of the Princess of Wales and the Queen's Jubilee celebrations. The aftermath in the USA of the terrorist attacks of 11 September 2001 includes examples of both civil and 'traditional' religion. Not only did many Americans turn to their church for comfort, but the attacks resulted in a wave of nationalism and patriotism which, according to some, served to bring Americans closer in a display of shared grief. It is not clear whether 'civil religion' is an example of religion losing its functions to other agencies, or whether religion has entered 'civil' life.

Another important evaluative paragraph introduces the concept of 'civil religion' with appropriate examples. The final sentence attempts to show the difficulties of interpreting the evidence.

In conclusion, it seems that there is no doubt that some of the functions once performed by religion and religious agencies are now performed by other bodies. However, this is not to say that religion has 'lost' its functions — indeed, for many people religion continues to perform a variety of functions and is an essential part of their life. There is also the argument that the remaining functions performed by religion have actually increased in importance.

This is a good conclusion which arises out of the preceding arguments and attempts to provide an answer to the question. The meaning of the last sentence could perhaps have been made clearer, possibly by use of an appropriate example.

Overall, the candidate has written a well-focused and sociologically sound answer displaying a good breadth of relevant knowledge, both theoretical and empirical, as well as the skills of interpretation, analysis and evaluation. There is appropriate use of examples, and both 'arguments' and 'evidence' are presented.

AO1: 20 + AO2: 17 = **37/40 marks**

Overall: 57/60 marks

■ ■ ■

Answer to question 3: grade-C candidate

(a) Some sects are short-lived because they prophesy something like the end of the world on a certain date and this doesn't happen. Some end up with all the members killing themselves like the Jonestown group or the Branch Davidians at Waco or Heaven's Gate.

🖉 This is an insufficient answer. Two possible reasons are identified (though not very clearly), namely a failing prophecy and the extreme situation of members committing suicide, but neither of these is explained. It is essential in questions such as this to make sure that you clearly 'identify' and 'explain'. At A2, you should be able to write at least three or four sentences by way of explanation. In addition, it is always a good idea to separate out your two reasons and explanations.

2 + 0 + 2 + 0 = **4/8 marks**

(b) As it says in Item A, fundamentalism is now found on a large scale and across several continents. Some sociologists say that this shows that secularisation is not taking place, because fundamentalists are very religious people who are fanatically committed to their religion.

🖉 This fairly weak introduction repeats some material from the source material, although some attempt is made to show the link to the secularisation debate.

Fundamentalism is when people believe that what is written in the holy books of the religion is true, such as in Christianity that Jesus could perform miracles and rose again from the dead. Not only do followers believe every word that is written, but they also try to live their life according to the 'rules' laid down in the holy book. The trouble with this is that sometimes there are contradictions, depending on which bit of the book you are reading, and you have to rely on the priests or holy men to interpret it for you.

🖉 A reasonable attempt is made to explain what fundamentalism is, and some interpretation and evaluation are brought into the discussion of possible problems with fundamentalist practices.

One reason for the rise in fundamentalism is that some people, especially religious leaders, believe that their religion and their people have been corrupted by bad influences, so they work very hard to make people go back to the original ways of believing and behaving. Sometimes they are able to do this just by preaching the message, such as parts of the New Christian Right in America, but sometimes they are able to force people to do this because they have gained power in that society, such as the Ayatollahs in Iran or the Taliban in Afghanistan.

 A reason is given for the rise in fundamentalism, supported by appropriate examples. A good distinction is made between situations in which people are 'persuaded' and those in which religious rules are able to be 'enforced'.

Another reason is that some people, especially immigrants, use their religion as part of their identity. This is true of some Muslim fundamentalists in Britain, and in extreme cases they may even join organisations such as Al Qaida and be prepared to fight for their beliefs. This can be linked to the fact that they might be discriminated against in Britain, suffering racism, and see their religion as a way of expressing their identity and even gaining status. Religion is able to compensate for the wrongs that they suffer in their everyday lives. They might also be attracted to the notion that if they follow all the rules of their religion to the letter, they will be rewarded in the afterlife. This is one way that some religious groups are able to get people prepared to sacrifice their lives for 'the cause', as they believe that this guarantees them a place in heaven.

 An attempt is made here to show a link between religion (though not always clearly focused on fundamentalism) and issues of national identity and 'compensation' for injustices in everyday life.

There probably isn't just one reason for the rise in fundamentalism, as it needs to be looked at in each particular society, taking into account the background. In times of change and upheaval where the old rules and ways of life have been disrupted (what Durkheim called anomie), people often look for something that gives them clear guidance about how to behave.

 There is potentially some good material here, and it is a pity that the reference to anomie isn't developed. There is a hint of evaluation in the recognition that there are probably different reasons for the rise in fundamentalism.

The candidate makes a reasonable attempt to answer part (b), though with occasional lack of focus. The material offered shows a basic knowledge and understanding of some of the issues, and there are a few explicit attempts at evaluation.

6/12 marks

(c) Durkheim and the functionalists believed that religion performed certain important functions for society. These included teaching moral values (right from wrong) and getting a sense of shared identity by taking part in communal rituals, such as praying together or attending ceremonies such as marriages and funerals or rites of passage when someone goes from one status to the next.

 An immediate link is made between the question and the functionalist perspective, and there is a brief but competent discussion of some of the functions of religion, together with examples.

However, while this may have been true in simple societies, or in modern societies in the past, some people claim that religion has become less important as it has 'lost' a lot of its functions, which are now performed by other institutions in society. In other words, society has become secularised, and not nearly as many people are influenced by religion as in the past. Sometimes this is from choice, such as when people make up their own mind about whether they should use contraception or not (even if they are Roman Catholic), but sometimes it is because the state has actually taken over the functions that religion used to perform.

🖉 The candidate expands the view expressed in the question, with a link to the notion of secularisation. The middle section wanders a little into people choosing not to be 'influenced' by religion, but gets back on track at the end with the reference to the state having taken over some of the functions of religion. This partial loss of focus can easily happen, especially when a powerful concept such as 'secularisation' is introduced. Make sure, particularly in the questions which are allocated fewer marks, that you do not lose sight of what the question is about — don't get side-tracked into another discussion.

Teaching people moral values can only be a function of religion if people are 'religious', i.e. if they go to church and learn from the religious teachers. As so many people don't ever go to church, or go very seldom, most people will get their moral values from elsewhere, such as their parents. Caring for the sick is now done by the NHS, and the state provides an education for all children. There are now professional counsellors to help people in times of trouble, whereas in the past they might have had to rely on the priests.

🖉 The candidate gives some examples of functions once performed by the church that are now performed by other agencies.

Another function of religion used to be that it offered explanations for why things happened, such as illness, death and disasters. As society has become more rational, and as scientific knowledge has increased, we now have other explanations for these phenomena, ones that can be shown to be true. For example, the foot and mouth outbreak in 2001 was not presented, even by priests, as something that happened because God was angry, but was shown to be the spread of an infectious disease affecting cattle. Similarly, most people accept that many of the world's natural disasters, such as forest fires and floods, are a result of global warming, not punishment from heaven. This information is made available to people by the state and other agencies such as the media. When people turn away from religious explanations to scientific ones it is known as 'disenchantment'.

🖉 A further discussion of one of the functions of religion being replaced by 'rational' thought and a belief in scientific explanations brings in the concept of 'disenchantment'. It is always a good idea to use as many relevant sociological concepts as possible. The discussion of 'rationality' could have been used to introduce some of the arguments referred to in the question. Remember that if the question asks for arguments and evidence, you must address both.

Does this mean that religion doesn't have any functions to perform for people or society? Obviously, religion is still important for some people, and such people would turn to their church for guidance, leadership and comfort in times of trouble. Some terrible events, such as the disaster on 11 September 2001 or the death of Princess Diana, still cause people to turn to the church, even those who might not usually go. The church can still offer comfort in times of trouble or national mourning. Religious leaders might not have much, if any, real political influence, but their views are still widely reported in the media and so reach many people.

💫 Some evaluation, largely implicit, is included in a discussion showing that religion does still have some functions to perform, with appropriate examples.

So, while it is true that religion has lost many of its functions, it is not true that it no longer has any. Religion can still reach people on an individual level in ways that the state and its agencies may not be able to. Secularisation may be taking place, but religion still has a place in our society.

💫 This is a reasonable conclusion with a hint of evaluation.

Although an acceptable level of sociological knowledge and understanding is demonstrated in part (c), there are some omissions, notably of any discussion of 'arguments' as opposed to 'evidence'. Similarly, there is no overt recognition of Britain as a multicultural society, which means that the opportunity is lost for evaluative points regarding those faiths that could be argued to have retained many of their functions. The interpretation of the question is broadly sociological, however, and there is evidence of some limited evaluation.

AO1: 11/20 + AO2: 9/20 = **20/40 marks**

Overall: 30/60 marks

Denominations; religiosity; religion as a conservative force

Item A

Belief in God: Great Britain 1998 (%)	
I know God really exists and I have no doubt about it.	21
While I have doubts, I feel that I do believe in God.	23
I find myself believing in God some of the time, but not at others.	14
I don't believe in a personal God, but I do believe in a Higher Power of some kind.	14
I don't believe there is a God and I don't believe there is any way to find out.	15
I don't believe in God.	10
Not answered	3
All	**100**

Source: *Social Trends*, No. 30, 2000.

(a) **Briefly outline the main characteristics of a denomination.** (8 marks)

(b) **With reference to Item A and elsewhere, examine some of the problems in measuring the degree of religiosity in society.** (12 marks)

(c) **Assess the view that religion inevitably acts as a conservative force in society.** (40 marks)

Total: 60 marks

■ ■ ■

Answer to question 4: grade-A candidate

(a) A 'denomination' is usually thought of as a religious organisation falling somewhere between a church and a sect, and sharing some of the characteristics of each. Some current denominations actually started off as sects, such as Quakers and Methodists, while some are formed when they 'break away' from established churches, showing that it is not always easy to classify religious organisations, other than as 'ideal types'.

> ✎ The candidate starts with a brief but relevant introduction showing good socio-logical knowledge. Remember that in short-answer questions carrying relatively few marks, it is important to get to the point and stick to it.

A denomination has voluntary membership by conversion rather than member-ship by birth. Larger denominations usually have a bureaucratic structure, like a church, but they are not always organised into a hierarchical structure, and some, such as the Quakers, do not have paid clergy. Denominations do not claim that they alone have the universal truth, and are tolerant of other religious beliefs and organisations.

> This is a well-focused list of some of the main characteristics of denominations. The fact that there are differences between denominations is also pointed out.

Denominations are also 'disengaged' from the state in that they do not fulfil any specific public or political functions, such as might be performed by the 'official' church, e.g. the Church of England. Some denominations are (or were) associated with particular social groups, such as the Methodists with their appeal to the newly industrialised English working class in the eighteenth and nineteenth centuries, and Southern Baptists in the USA who draw a large part of their congregations from the poorer black community.

> Further focused and relevant knowledge is combined with specific examples to illustrate the points made. There is no formal conclusion to the answer, but this is less of a problem in a short-answer question such as this than in a 40-mark essay.
>
> The information provided in part (a) is relevant, well-informed, sociological and to the point. **8/8 marks**

(b) The kind of information shown in Item A is often used alongside information demonstrating a decline in membership of religious organisations. Looking at the table, we can see that 72% of respondents had some belief in God or a 'Higher Power', while only 25% said that they had no belief in God. This apparent contradiction between the small percentage of people who are members of some kind of church and those who have a spiritual belief illustrates what Grace Davie has called 'believing, not belonging'.

> The answer makes immediate and relevant use of Item A, interpreting the information contained in the table and using it to make an important sociological point. Remember always to *use* the information in the item, and not simply to copy it out or even ignore it altogether.

The high proportion of people claiming to have a spiritual belief is often used as evidence of a high degree of religiosity, which goes against the view that secularisation is taking place. However, one of the problems is that there is no agreement on what we actually mean by 'religiosity' and therefore how this should be measured.

> The answer then homes in on the concept of 'religiosity'. It is important in shorter answers to focus on the set question as early as possible — there is no room for irrelevant material. Here the important point of there being no agreed definition of religiosity is also made, and is linked to a problem of measurement.

The method of measuring religiosity used by the authors of Item A is to ask people about their level of spiritual belief. This methodology has the same weakness as all surveys, namely that it is impossible to know whether people are telling the truth. Some people, faced with questions about their religious belief, might become superstitious and feel that it would be 'unlucky' to deny a belief in God. This could lead them to claim a religiosity that they didn't really feel, skewing the figures to show a higher than true percentage. On the other side of the equation, if the survey included people from non-Christian faiths, they might have answered negatively because talk of 'God' or even a 'Higher Power' might be inappropriate. In this case the figures would show a lower than true 'religiosity'. However, it is difficult to see how religiosity, when defined in terms of a spiritual belief rather than religious practice, could be measured in any other way than by asking people in a survey.

☑ The focus on the question is maintained by a brief discussion of one possible way of measuring religiosity together with a couple of problems, thus showing both appropriate knowledge and understanding, and some evaluation.

There is obviously a gap, as indicated by Item A, between the proportion of people expressing a religious belief, and the proportion of people involved in some kind of measurable religious practice, such as going to worship. But is just saying that you have a belief in God or some spiritual being really 'religiosity'? It could be argued that having this belief isn't really worth much if it isn't backed up by some kind of religious practice. Taking just the Christian faith, the growing commercialisation of Christmas seems to show that for most people there are few, if any, links between the parties, presents and celebrations and the religious significance of the festival. A recent survey showed that many people didn't even know what the religious significance of Easter was.

☑ Another appropriate reference is made to the source material, and further analytical/evaluation skills are shown by the brief discussion about what is really meant by 'religiosity'. Two interesting examples are given to cast further doubt on the significance of the term.

To sum up, most of the problems of measuring the degree of religiosity in society stem from the fact that there is no agreed definition of the term. Further problems arise if we try to argue that a belief in God shows that people are actually 'religious'. Perhaps 'believing' needs to be linked to 'belonging' before we can argue that secularisation is not taking place.

☑ This interesting conclusion not only sums up the preceding arguments but places them in the context of the secularisation debate.

This is a well-focused and well-argued answer with appropriate reference to the source material. It would have benefited from some reference to sociological theory — try to think of a couple of appropriate points that could have been made in this respect. **10/12 marks**

(c) The view that religion acts as a conservative force in society is usually linked to Marxism. Marx argued that the bourgeoisie used religious ideas as part of the 'ideological state apparatus', that is, those institutions that served to conceal the capitalist exploitation of the working class and at the same time make them (falsely) believe that society was fair and meritocratic.

> ✐ A strong introduction immediately places the view expressed in the question in an appropriate sociological context and begins to offer an explanation of it. It is always a good idea to show that you can associate a particular viewpoint with a theory or perspective, even if later you show how things are perhaps more complex than they seem at first.

With regard to religion, Marx attempted to show how religious beliefs were linked to those holding power in society, and how they were used to justify the unequal amounts not only of power but also of wealth and status in society. Traditionally, religion is also linked to 'worthwhile' knowledge, and there are many examples of how important knowledge in society is guarded by the 'priestly class', such as when priests or monks hold the important books in their libraries and even control levels of literacy. The effect of this is that power and privilege in society tend to stay with those who already have them, a position justified by the dominant religion. This leads to religion being a conservative force, in that religious beliefs tend to work against any significant changes taking place, at least in terms of who has the power.

> ✐ There is potentially some very good material here, though the meaning is not always as clear as it might be. The points being made would have benefited from being supported by some actual examples. Try to think of one or two that could have been used — for example, of societies where priests or monks hold or held the 'important books', or particular religious beliefs which justify the existing hierarchy in society.

An example that is often offered to demonstrate how religion can act as a conservative force in society is that of the Hindu caste system. This existed for two thousand years, and the huge inequalities between the different castes were explained, justified and maintained by religious beliefs, particularly that of reincarnation. Put simply, this meant that Hindus believed that only if they obeyed the rules of their caste to the letter would they be reincarnated into a higher caste. Failure to obey caste rules also resulted in punishment in this life, not just in the afterlife, with offenders having to go through ritual purification to be reinstated, or, if the offence was too serious for this, becoming 'out-castes' and not being able to live with the group. Even those right at the bottom of the society, the 'untouchables', had an incentive to put up with their lot uncomplainingly, in expectation of being one rung up the caste ladder in the next life. Although the caste was outlawed by the British under colonial rule in India, it still persisted, especially in rural areas, and the length of time it lasted is an outstanding example of how religious ideas can act as a conservative force in society.

> ✐ This is a rather long paragraph, though it provides an example that is relevant to the question. Try to see how it could be made a little shorter without losing any of the essential points.

However, it could be argued that Durkheim also views religion as a conservative force. For Durkheim, religion acts as the 'moral glue' that holds a society together, and its rituals and teachings help to reinforce the shared norms and values that he believed were essential to keep society free from destructive conflict. Durkheim, in fact, also believed that religion served to maintain the inequalities in society, but while Marx saw this as a bad thing, Durkheim saw it in a positive light, since acceptance of inequality reduced the chance of conflict. Marx thought that revolutionary conflict would be a good thing, as it would destroy capitalism and the bourgeoisie, while Durkheim saw conflict as bad, as it risked destroying the 'conscience collective' that was at the basis of society.

✓ The discussion is widened to take in a further perspective, namely Durkheimian functionalism, and some interesting points of comparison are made between the views of Marx and Durkheim.

However, is it true that religion 'inevitably' acts as a conservative force? The evidence suggests that this is not the case. Weber, for example, in his work 'The Protestant Ethic and the Spirit of Capitalism', showed how the early Calvinists saw work as a 'calling' which they should follow with all their efforts, as by doing so they were honouring God. These efforts, together with their belief in the need for a lifestyle without any form of luxury, led to them amassing large amounts of money, which were then used for investment in the mills, mines and factories of early capitalism. Weber thus argued that, while Calvinist beliefs did not cause capitalism, the practices which followed from those beliefs helped industrial capitalism to 'take off'. There is thus a link in this case between a particular kind of religious belief and huge social change.

✓ This is a good analytical summary of the link between the Protestant work ethic and the development of capitalism which avoids the common mistake of claiming that Weber argued that one was caused by the other. The view that religion 'inevitably' acts as a conservative force is challenged by this evidence, thus displaying evaluation.

Another example would be Islamic fundamentalist revolutionary movements, such as that led by the Ayatollah Khomenei, which overthrew the ruling family in Iran and established a fundamentalist state. Another example of religion wishing to bring about social change is the radical Islamic movement, the Nation of Islam, which was closely associated with the civil rights movement in America. Followers were taught that they should reclaim Islam as their cultural birthright and take their rightful place in society, and should resist being treated as slaves and 'second-class citizens' by whites. The aim of the Nation of Islam is black segregation, with followers living in their own self-sufficient society, with a strict moral code. Their leader, Louis Farrakhan, was banned from entering Britain as it was believed that his presence would lead to scenes of public disorder.

✓ A strong paragraph presents evidence against the view that religion 'inevitably' acts as a conservative force, using good examples to support the argument. The

question

candidate is again demonstrating critical and evaluative skills, as well as relevant knowledge and understanding.

Finally, the so-called 'liberation theology' of South America, where radical Roman Catholic priests and nuns taught that it was the people's duty to rise up against oppression, is a further example to show that religious ideas can be associated with social change.

✐ A further example is offered as a critique of the view expressed in the question.

In conclusion, the evidence suggests that in many cases religion does act as a conservative force in society, helping to maintain the status quo and prevent change, particularly revolutionary social change. However, other evidence suggests that there is nothing 'inevitable' about this process, and that religious ideas can also be associated, sometimes quite strongly, with a move for social change.

✐ This succinct conclusion returns to the set question and accurately summarises the arguments put forward in the main body of the answer.

This is a strong answer to part (c) with both a theoretical and empirical focus. It answers the question, and makes good use of relevant examples to support the arguments. Some of the points could perhaps have been made more briefly, but if a student is able to present a fuller answer to all parts of the question within the time allowed, and provided that the information is relevant to the question, lengthiness is not necessarily a problem. This emphasises the importance of writing timed answers to (unseen) questions, so that you can learn approximately how much you are able to write in the time allowed. The skills of interpretation, analysis and evaluation are present here, though perhaps not displayed as strongly as the AO1 skills.   AO1: 20/20 + AO2: 17/20 = **37/40 marks**

Overall: 55/60 marks

■ ■ ■

Answer to question 4: grade-C candidate

(a) A denomination falls somewhere between a church and a sect. Denominations have a hierarchical structure and a professional clergy but also use 'lay' people as preachers. Denominations are tolerant of other faiths and do not say that only they have the 'truth'. They are separate from the state but support its aims. Denominations usually have a middle-class membership.

✐ This introduction lists points rather abruptly but still identifies a range of characteristics associated with denominations. As the question asked for a 'brief outline', this is acceptable, though a slightly fuller answer, perhaps with some examples of denominations or pointing out that there are some differences between them, would have been better.   **5/8 marks**

(b) Item A shows that only 25% of people in the survey said they didn't believe in God. This goes against the idea that secularisation is taking place in Britain. Secularisation is when religious thinking, practices and organisations lose their social significance. If 75% of the population believe in God, as the table shows, then this doesn't support the idea that Britain is becoming a secular society.

> ✍ While reference is made to Item A, and some appropriate material is extracted and used, it is not accurate to state that the table shows that 75% of the population (which population?) believe in God. Why not? There appears to be a danger that this answer is going to focus on 'secularisation' rather than 'religiosity'.

Not all sociologists agree that secularisation is taking place. Martin says that we shouldn't look back to a 'Golden Age' of religion and say that we are not as religious now as we were then, as there was no such 'Golden Age' and priests have always had problems with getting people to go to church. So, according to Martin, we are not necessarily less 'religious' than we were. However, Wilson and Bruce believe that secularisation is taking place, and say that there is not as much religiosity as there was in the past.

> ✍ This paragraph illustrates a common problem — namely that the student has lost track of the focus of the question, and is answering a different one. This question is not about whether secularisation is taking place; it is about the problems of measuring the degree of 'religiosity' in society. The focus should therefore be on the meaning of 'religiosity' and on methodological issues. Do not begin to write an answer until you have clearly fixed in your mind what the question is actually asking you to do.

One way of measuring religiosity is to find out how many people go to church. There are problems with this, as there can be double-counting, counting might only be done at Easter or Christmas, or priests might exaggerate the number of people they attract to their services in order to please the bishop. Another way is asking people if they have a religious belief, as in Item A. This is probably a better way, as you can be religious without going to church. Item A shows that three-quarters of people believe in God, therefore there is a high degree of religiosity in society and secularisation is probably not taking place.

> ✍ A belated focus on the issues of 'religiosity' and 'measurement' is only partially successful. Two possible ways of measuring religiosity are offered, with some problems of measurement being stated for the first, though not explained. The second point repeats the error in interpreting the table, and returns to the issue of secularisation, thus losing the focus again. The only evaluative points are the weak references to church attendance statistics. **5/12 marks**

(c) Marx believed that religion acted as a conservative force in society. Marxists say that religion is part of the ideological state apparatus, and helps to keep the bourgeoisie in power by getting the masses to believe that it is God's will that some people should be rich and powerful and others should be poor and power-less. This is shown in the Victorian hymn:

The rich man in his castle
The poor man at his gate
God made them high and lowly
And ordered their estate.

> There is an immediate link between the question and the Marxist perspective, with some knowledge of the Marxist view of religion. Many students choose to quote the verse above in their answers. At least in this case it is linked to the point being made, but as a general rule, it is not necessary to quote the verse in full. It could, however, be useful to point out that there are many hymns which make reference to social inequalities being 'God-given', together with the assumption that people should therefore accept willingly these inequalities and not question them.

Marx also said that religion was the 'opium of the people', which meant that it was like a drug, and helped them to cope with the pain and suffering in their life brought about by their exploitation. If religion acts as opium, deadening the pain, then this is also helping to stop social change, as the masses will have some comfort from their suffering and be able to put up with it.

> The candidate demonstrates further relevant knowledge and understanding of the Marxist view, linked to the notion of religion acting as a conservative force. So far, there is a much better focus on the question than there was in part (b).

The Indian caste system also shows how religion can act as a conservative force in society. Because everyone was taught by their religion that the only way to come back in the next life in a higher caste was to obey all the caste rules, the hierarchy stayed unchanged for over a thousand years.

> This is a further relevant example of religion acting as a conservative force in society.

However, Weber thought that religion was not conservative but could also be used to bring about social change. In his book 'The Protestant Ethic and the Spirit of Capitalism', Weber showed how the beliefs of the Calvinists caused capitalism, which was, of course, a huge social change. Calvinists didn't believe in spending money on luxuries and worked very hard, so they were able to save huge amounts of money and invested this in the new mills and factories, helping to bring about modern capitalism. This is an example of religion not being conservative but bringing about social change.

> The discussion of Weber provides a good illustration of the link between religious beliefs and social change, but this is not properly explained or developed, and includes the common mistake of claiming that Weber argued that Calvinist beliefs 'caused' capitalism. If you are not sure of the actual arguments used by Weber, make sure that you revise these. There is no clear indication either of how the Calvinists' behaviour stemmed from their religious beliefs (make sure that you look

up 'predestination' in this context). Although the answer gives the title of Weber's book, there is no discussion of what is meant by the 'Protestant ethic'.

Liberation theology is another example of religion and social change, as priests taught that people should resist exploitation and try to change society. The Civil Rights movement and Black Power are also linked to religion, and these are trying to change society to make things better for black people.

Two further examples are given of links between religion and social change, but neither is developed. What else could have been included here to make the points clearer and more explicit?

The evidence about religion and social change is therefore not clear. There is evidence that religion does prevent social change in some circumstances, but also cases where religion works to bring about social change.

This fairly weak conclusion does not really add anything to what has gone before. However, the point about the evidence 'not being clear' shows an attempt to 'assess' the view expressed in the question.

The answer to part (c) shows a reasonably good knowledge of some relevant sociological material with some inaccuracies. The knowledge is both theoretical and empirical, and there is a focus on the question. There is little analysis, and evaluation is largely by juxtaposition, but the question is interpreted in a socio-logical manner.   AO1: 12/20 + AO2: 7/20 = **19/40 marks**

Overall: 29/60 marks

New Religious Movements; sects; religion and science

Item A

One of the characteristics of the modern world is the growing reliance on science. Scientific and technological explanations increasingly take precedence over religious ones, and most people have greater faith in the scientific expert than in the priest. The 'sacred canopy' of religion that helped people to understand and make sense of their everyday life has been replaced by a system of legal-rational rules and authority, and political and economic forces are now believed to have far more influence than religious ones. Rational thought and scientific explanations have replaced beliefs in magic and superstitions, and religious beliefs and practices, where they still exist, are personal and confined to the private sphere of life.

(a) **Identify and briefly explain two reasons for the growth of New Religious Movements.** (8 marks)

(b) **Examine some of the problems involved in identifying the characteristics of a sect.** (12 marks)

(c) **Using information from Item A and elsewhere, assess the view that 'scientific and technological explanations increasingly take precedence over religious ones'.** (40 marks)

Total: 60 marks

■ ■ ■

The question above is one for you to try yourself. The notes below are offered as guidance, but you should work out yourself how best to answer the question, and do your own research. The best way of using this question is to decide how you are going to answer each part, check on any information you are not sure about and make a brief plan for parts (b) and (c). Then allow yourself 1 hour 30 minutes of uninterrupted time, put your books away, set the timer and write your answer. Remember to leave yourself sufficient time to read through your answer to correct any mistakes.

(a) Decide what your two reasons are going to be. Take each one in turn, state it clearly and then write two or three sentences explaining clearly why it is a reason for the growth of NRMs. Separate out the two parts of the answer by leaving a line, so that an examiner could see clearly that you have identified and explained two separate reasons.

(b) One way to tackle this is to see whether you can identify any characteristics that are common to all sects — is there an 'ideal type'? As the question implies, there are problems with attempting to identify the characteristics of sects, so you will need to decide what some of these problems are. (In a 12-mark question, you are not expected to be able to discuss everything that might be relevant, so try to pick out some of the main points.) Obviously, one of the problems is going to be that there are different kinds of sect, so you will need to discuss this point. Remember to illustrate your answer with appropriate examples.

(c) Read the source material carefully, and try to summarise in your mind what it is saying. Identify any key concepts that you will need to refer to in your answer. Think about whether there is a particular sociological concept that may not have been used in the passage, but which applies to the process it is describing. If so, is this concept associated with a particular sociologist or perspective?

Now decide what arguments and evidence could be put forward in support of the view expressed in Item A. What examples could you use in defence of the view?

Having done this, take the opposing position, and decide where there are arguments and evidence that could be used against the view. Again, find examples to illustrate your points. Remember (as with all questions on religion) that you do not need to confine your answer to modern Britain, but that wherever you do talk about Britain it should be as a multicultural and multifaith society, so make sure that your answer does not focus exclusively on evidence drawn from just one particular faith.

Finally, look back at your evidence and arguments to see whether you are able to come to a definite conclusion regarding the validity of the view expressed in Item A. Sometimes it is possible to come to a clear conclusion, but at other times it is not. Often, the answer to the question depends on factors such as the meaning given to particular terms, how different pieces of evidence are interpreted, or on the perspective taken by particular sociologists. However, if this is the case, these points should be briefly summarised in your conclusion, so that the reason that you have not been able to come to a definite answer is clearly indicated to the examiner.